Low **FOD MAP** Diet Cookbook

A Comprehensive Low FOD MAP Guide and Recipe Book Delight Your Taste Buds with Healthy and Nutritious Delicacies for Soothe Your Gut and Overcome IBS. 31 Day Meal Plan Included.

Olivia Green

Table of Contents

Introduction to Low FODMAP diet...7

    What is IBS?...7

    The Role of FODMAPs 8

    What Are Low-FODMAP Foods?...8

How Does the Low-FODMAP Diet Work?..9

    The Science Behind the Low-FODMAP Diet 9

    How to Living with IBS: Practical Strategies 10

Foods to Avoid..11

Foods to Eat..12

Juices & Smoothies Recipes...13

    Strawberry Juice...14

    Blueberry Juice 14

    Cranberry & Orange Juice..15

    Grapes Juice...15

    Grapes & Strawberry Juice 16

    Papaya Juice...16

    Pineapple Juice 17

    Orange Juice 17

    Spinach & Cucumber Juice..18

    Kale & Celery Juice...18

    Protein Smoothie 19

    Coffee Banana Smoothie 19

    Raspberry Tofu Smoothie 20

    Strawberry Smoothie 20

    Papaya Smoothie..21

    Matcha Smoothie 21

    Spinach & Lettuce Smoothie...22

    Kale & Celery Smoothie 22

    Cucumber & Parsley Smoothie..23

    Green Veggies Smoothie 23

Breakfast Recipes..24

Acai Smoothie Bowl 25

Strawberry Smoothie Bowl 25

Cheese & Yoghurt Bowl 26

Strawberry Chia Pudding 26

Blueberry Oatmeal 27

Oatmeal Yoghurt Bowl 27

Overnight Seeds Porridge 28

Quinoa Porridge 29

Buckwheat Porridge 30

Bulgur Porridge 31

Maple Pancakes 32

Banana Waffles 33

Blueberry Muffins 34

Courgette Bread 35

Oats & Quinoa Granola 36

Tomato & Egg Scramble 37

Salmon Omelet 38

Green Veggies Quiche 39

Chicken & Veggies Frittata 40

Eggs with Beef & Tomatoes 41

Lunch Recipes 42

Egg Salad 43

Raspberry Salad 43

Courgette & Tomato Salad 44

Veggie Lettuce Wraps 44

Chicken Lettuce Wraps 46

Beef Burgers 47

Turkey Meatballs 48

Egg Drop Soup 49

Tomato Soup 50

Stuffed Capsicums 51

Stuffed Courgette 52

Chicken & Veggie Kabobs 53

Spiced Ground Chicken 54

Chicken Gizzard with Cabbage 55

Turkey Meatloaf 56

Shrimp with Kale 57

Scallops with Green Beans 58

Banana Curry 59

Spinach with Cottage Cheese 60

Tofu with Broccoli 61

Dinner Recipes 62

Chicken Salad 63

Pork Salad 64

Salmon Salad 64

Ground Beef & Cabbage Soup 65

Lentil Soup 66

Pork Stew 67

Shrimp Stew 68

Chickpeas Stew 69

Turkey & Beans Chili 70

Chickpeas & Courgette Chili 71

Chicken & Broccoli Curry 72

Parmesan Chicken Bake 73

Braised Chicken Thighs 74

Ground Turkey with Veggies 75

Herbed Flank Steak 76

Pork with Pineapple 77

Salmon Parcel 78

Haddock with Tomatoes 79

Seafood Casserole 80

Noodles with Chicken & Veggies 81

Snacks Recipes 82

Spiced Pecans 83

Cinnamon Popcorn 84

Banana Chips 84

Sweet Potato Fries 85

Deviled Eggs 86

Almond Brittles 87

Parmesan Shrimp 88

Chicken Popcorn 89

Berries Gazpacho 90

Stuffed Cherry Tomatoes 90

Dessert Recipes 91

Lemon Sorbet 92

Blueberry Gelato 93

Berries Granita 94

Raspberry Mousse 94

Blueberry Pudding 95

Cottage Cheese Pudding 96

Lemon Soufflé 97

Egg Custard 98

Peanut Butter Fudge 99

Pumpkin Brownies 100

Blueberry Crumble 101

31 Days Meal Plan 102

Introduction to Low FODMAP diet

Are you aware that the low-FODMAP diet can help you minimize certain carbohydrates that make it difficult for your system to digest properly? Usually, it is a strategic approach that healthcare professionals recommend as an elimination diet to identify food triggers in people who have functional gastrointestinal disorders, such as IBS.

However, living with Irritable Bowel Syndrome (IBS) could be challenging, marked by discomfort and uncertainty. If you are suffering from this condition, I am happy to inform you that there is hope. And the low-FODMAP diet is the answer.

In this comprehensive guide, you will get to understand what low-FODMAP foods are, how they can benefit people with IBS, the science behind IBS, and practical strategies for incorporating this diet into your daily life. With this knowledge, you can rest assured that you will have improved digestive health and quality of life.

Now, let's get into the nitty gritty of this guide.

What is IBS?

Irritable Bowel Syndrome, or IBS, is a gastrointestinal disorder that affects millions of people globally. It has a myriad of distressing and unpleasant symptoms, which include abdominal pain, bloating, gas, diarrhea, and constipation. Basically, it is a kind of disorder that affects our intestines and stomach. What makes IBS particularly perplexing is its elusive nature – no research has established its exact cause. And so far, there is no one-size-fits-all cure for it. However, some recent developments in our understanding of IBS have clarified the role of certain dietary components in triggering and exacerbating its symptoms.

The Role of FODMAPs

The next essential thing to discuss is the role of FODMAPs. But before we go deeper, what does it even mean? It simply stands for Fermentable Oligosaccharides, Disaccharides, Monosaccharides, and Polyols. They are a group of carbohydrates found in a variety of foods. These compounds have been identified as potential culprits in triggering IBS symptoms.

Anytime FODMAPs reach the small intestine undigested, they draw excess water into the bowel and ferment, which leads to gas production and bloating. Additionally, these fermentable carbohydrates serve as a food source for gut bacteria, contributing to the development of IBS symptoms.

What Are Low-FODMAP Foods?

The low-FODMAP diet is a dietary approach designed to get rid of the symptoms of IBS. It has to do with minimizing the consumption of foods high in FODMAPs and substituting them with options that are low in these fermentable carbohydrates. By doing so, individuals with IBS can reduce the potential triggers for their symptoms. Consequently, they will be relieved.

Low-FODMAP foods primarily consist of:

- Protein Sources: These include meat, fish, and tofu are generally low in FODMAPs and can serve as excellent sources of protein for those following the diet.

- Gluten-Free Grains: Examples of grains that are kind to the gut and suitable for a low-FODMAP eating plan include rice, oats, and quinoa.

- Certain Fruits and Vegetables: While many fruits and vegetables are high in FODMAPs, there are exceptions such as carrots, spinach, and blueberries. These fruits and vegetables mentioned can only be enjoyed moderately.

- Lactose-Free Dairy: Lactose is a type of disaccharide that triggers symptoms in people with IBS. Opting for lactose-free dairy products is a smart choice for those following the low-FODMAP diet.

How Does the Low-FODMAP Diet Work?

The fundamental principle of the low-FODMAP diet is to limit the intake of foods that can exacerbate IBS symptoms. This approach is categorized into three phases:

- Elimination Phase: During this phase, you should avoid high-FODMAP foods for a specified period, usually 2 to 6 weeks. This helps to identify which FODMAPs trigger your symptoms.

- Reintroduction Phase: Once you are done with the elimination phase, FODMAPs are gradually reintroduced one at a time to determine which specific carbohydrates are problematic in your system. This phase is essential for personalizing the diet you need.

- Maintenance Phase: In this last phase, you should establish a long-term eating plan that minimizes FODMAPs while allowing for a varied and balanced diet.

The Science Behind the Low-FODMAP Diet

Do you know that the potency of the low-FODMAP diet is supported by scientific research? Multiple studies have revealed its effectiveness in reducing IBS symptoms, particularly in individuals with a subtype known as IBS-D (IBS with diarrhea) and IBS-M (IBS with mixed symptoms).

The mechanism behind the diet's success lies in its ability to minimize the fermentable carbohydrates that can cause gut distress. By limiting FODMAP intake, you can achieve a significant reduction in abdominal pain, bloating, and altered bowel habits.

How to Living with IBS: Practical Strategies

Living with IBS and following a low-FODMAP diet might be challenging at first. But with the appropriate strategies, it can become a manageable and even interesting part of your daily life. Below are what you can do:

- Consult a Registered Dietitian: You should consider working with a registered dietitian who specializes in IBS and the Low-FODMAP diet can be invaluable. They can help you create a customized meal plan. Also, they will guide you through the various phases of the diet.

- Read Labels: Understanding food labels and identifying FODMAP-containing ingredients is essential. So, you have to look out for terms like fructose, lactose, and sorbitol, which are indicators of high-FODMAP foods.

- Plan and Prepare: Meal planning and preparation are vital to success. Stock your kitchen with low-FODMAP ingredients, and plan your meals ahead of time to avoid dietary pitfalls.

- Pay Attention to Your Symptoms: You need to keep a food diary to track your dietary intake and corresponding symptoms. This can help you identify triggers and make informed choices.

- Stay Informed: You must stay updated on the latest research and developments in the field of IBS and the low-FODMAP diet. Knowledge is power when it comes to managing your condition.

In conclusion, living with IBS can be a daunting journey, but the low-FODMAP diet offers hope and relief for you. Once you understand the role of FODMAPs in triggering IBS symptoms and embrace the principles of this dietary approach, you can take control of your digestive health and have a more comfortable, symptom-free life. You should also bear in mind that IBS is a highly individualized condition, and what works best for one person might be totally different from another. So, you should be intentional about working closely with healthcare professionals and a dietitian to tailor the low-FODMAP diet to your specific needs. With patience, knowledge, determination, and instruction, you can pave the way to a healthier and happier life, even in the face of IBS.

Foods to Avoid

Vegetables:

- **Garlic and Onions:** High in fructans, a type of oligosaccharides, leading to bloating and gas.

Fruits:

- **Apples and Pears:** These fruits are high in fructose, a monosaccharide that can be difficult to absorb, leading to gastrointestinal issues.

Protein:

- **Sausages and Processed Meats:** Often contain garlic and onion for flavoring and are high in unhealthy fats.

Grains:

- **Wheat and Rye:** Contain fructans and are major sources of gastrointestinal discomfort for sensitive individuals.

Dairy:

- **Milk and Soft Cheese:** High in lactose, a disaccharide that can cause bloating, gas, and diarrhea in sensitive individuals.

Foods to Eat

Vegetables:

- **Carrots and Zucchini:** These are low in FODMAPs and rich in essential nutrients that aid digestion and overall well-being.

Fruits:

- **Bananas and Strawberries:** These fruits are low in FODMAPs and a good source of dietary fiber, promoting regular bowel movements.

Protein:

- **Eggs and Chicken:** High in protein and low in FODMAPs, essential for muscle repair and growth without causing gastrointestinal discomfort.

Grains:

- **Rice and Oats:** These grains lack the fermentable carbohydrates, making them easy to digest and energy-providing.

Dairy:

- **Lactose-Free Milk and Hard Cheese:** They're low in lactose, reducing the risk of bloating and gas.

Juices & Smoothies Recipes

Strawberry Juice

Servings | 4   Time | 10 minutes
Nutritional Content (per serving):
Cal | 23   Fat | 0.2g   Protein | 0.5g   Carbs | 5.5g   Fibre | 1.4g

Ingredients:

- ❖ 250 grams (2 cups) fresh strawberries, hulled
- ❖ 5 millilitres (1 teaspoon) fresh lime juice
- ❖ 480 millilitres (2 cups) chilled water

Directions:

1. Put strawberries and remnant ingredients into a high-power mixer and process thoroughly.
2. Through a strainer, strain the juice and transfer into four glasses.
3. Enjoy immediately.

Blueberry Juice

Servings | 4   Time | 10 minutes
Nutritional Content (per serving):
Cal | 41   Fat | 0.2g   Protein | 0.4g   Carbs | 10g   Fibre | 1.1g

Ingredients:

- ❖ 190 grams (1¼ cups) fresh blueberries
- ❖ 2 grams (½ teaspoon) baking soda
- ❖ 15 millilitres (1 tablespoon) fresh lemon juice
- ❖ Ice cubes, as required
- ❖ 15 millilitres (1 tablespoon) white vinegar
- ❖ 20-40 grams (1-2 tablespoons) pure maple syrup
- ❖ 240 millilitres (1 cup) water

Directions:

1. Put vinegar and baking soda into a large-sized bowl of water and blend to incorporate thoroughly.
2. Put in blueberries and soak them for 15-20 minutes.
3. Drain the blueberries and rinse them thoroughly.
4. Again, drain the blueberries.
5. Put the blueberries, lemon juice, maple syrup and water into a high-power mixer and process to form a smooth mixture.
6. Divide the ice cubes into four glasses.
7. Through a fine mesh strainer, strain the juice into glasses and enjoy immediately.

Cranberry & Orange Juice

Servings | 4   Time | 10 minutes
Nutritional Content (per serving):
Cal | 71   Fat | 0.1g   Protein | 0.2g   Carbs | 15g   Fibre | 2.1g

Ingredients:

- ❖ 200 grams (2 cups) fresh cranberries
- ❖ 120 millilitres (½ cup) fresh orange juice
- ❖ 40 grams 40 grams (2 tablespoons) pure maple syrup
- ❖ Ice cubes, as required
- ❖ 120 millilitres 120 millilitres (½ cup) water
- ❖ 10 millilitres (2 teaspoons) fresh lemon juice

Directions:

1. Put the cranberries, water, orange juice, lemon juice and maple syrup into a high-power mixer and process to form a smooth mixture.
2. Put the ice cubes into two glasses.
3. Through a fine mesh strainer, strain the juice and transfer it into glasses over ice.
4. Enjoy immediately.

Grapes Juice

Servings | 4   Time | 10 minutes
Nutritional Content (per serving):
Cal | 61   Fat | 0g   Protein | 1g   Carbs | 14.2g   Fibre | 1.1g

Ingredients:

- ❖ 300 grams (2 cups) seedless red grapes
- ❖ 480 millilitres (2 cups) water
- ❖ ½ lime

Directions:

1. Into a high-power mixer Put and remnant ingredients and process thoroughly
2. Through a strainer, strain the juice and transfer into four glasses.
3. Enjoy immediately.

Grapes & Strawberry Juice

Servings | 4   Time | 10 minutes
Nutritional Content (per serving):
Cal | 50   Fat | 0.1g   Protein | 0.7g   Carbs | 11.9g   Fibre | 1.1g

Ingredients:

- 115 grams (4 ounces) fresh strawberries, hulled
- 5 grams (1 tablespoon) fresh mint leaves
- 180 millilitres (¾ cup) water
- Ice cubes, as required
- 85 grams (3 ounces) seedless red grapes
- 55 grams (2 ounces) seedless green grapes
- 10 millilitres (2 teaspoons) fresh lime juice
- 20 grams (1 tablespoon) pure maple syrup

Directions:

1. Put the strawberries, grapes mint leaves, lime juice, water and maple syrup into a high-power mixer and process to form a smooth mixture
2. Divide the ice cubes into four glasses.
3. Through a fine mesh strainer, strain the juice and transfer it into glasses over ice.
4. Enjoy immediately.

Papaya Juice

Servings | 4   Time | 10 minutes
Nutritional Content (per serving):
Cal | 45   Fat | 0.2g   Protein | 0.4g   Carbs | 11.3g   Fibre | 1.3g

Ingredients:

- 290 grams (2 cups) ripe papaya, peel, seeds removed and cut into chunks
- 120-180 millilitres (½-¾ cup) water
- 15 millilitres (1 tablespoon) fresh lemon juice
- Ice cubes, as required

Directions:

1. Put the papaya, maple syrup, lemon juice and water into a high-power mixer and process to form a smooth mixture.
2. Divide the ice cubes into two glasses.
3. Through a fine mesh strainer, strain the juice and transfer it into glasses over ice
4. Enjoy immediately.

Pineapple Juice

Servings | 4   Time | 10 minutes
Nutritional Content (per serving):
Cal | 41   Fat | 0.1g   Protein | 0.4g   Carbs | 10.8g   Fibre | 1.2g

Ingredients:

- ❖ 340 grams (2 cups) pineapple, peel removed and cut up
- ❖ 360 millilitres (1½ cups) water

Directions:

1. Put pineapple and water into a high-power mixer and process thoroughly.
2. Through a strainer, strain the juice and transfer into four glasses.
3. Enjoy immediately.

Orange Juice

Servings | 4   Time | 10 minutes
Nutritional Content (per serving):
Cal | 91   Fat | 0.2g   Protein | 1.3g   Carbs | 22.9g   Fibre | 3.3g

Ingredients:

- ❖ 3 oranges, peel removed and sectioned
- ❖ 240 millilitres (1 cup) water
- ❖ 40 grams (2 tablespoons) pure maple syrup
- ❖ Ice cubes, as required

Directions:

1. Put the orange sections, maple syrup and water into a high-power mixer and process to form a smooth mixture
2. Divide the ice cubes into four glasses.
3. Through a fine mesh strainer, strain the juice and transfer it into glasses over ice.
4. Enjoy immediately.

Spinach & Cucumber Juice

Servings|4 Time|10 minutes
Nutritional Content (per serving):
Cal| 48   Fat| 0.3g   Protein| 2g   Carbs| 11.5g   Fibre| 2g

Ingredients:

- 90 grams (3 cups) fresh spinach
- 2 grapefruits, peel removed, sectioned and seeds removed
- 2 large-sized cucumbers, cut into chunks
- 240 millilitres (1 cup) water
- Ice cubes, as required

Directions:

1. Put spinach, cucumbers, grapefruits and water into a high-power mixer and process to form a smooth mixture
2. Divide the ice cubes into two glasses.
3. Through a fine mesh strainer, strain the juice and transfer into four glasses over ice.
4. Enjoy immediately.

Kale & Celery Juice

Servings|4 Time|10 minutes
Nutritional Content (per serving):
Cal| 70   Fat| 0.1g   Protein| 4.1g   Carbs| 15g   Fibre| 2.3g

Ingredients:

- 2 celery stalks
- 5 grams (1 teaspoon) fresh ginger, peel removed
- 440 grams (8 cups) fresh kale leaves
- 1 lime, halved
- 120-240 millilitres (½-1 cup) water

Directions:

1. Put celery and remnant ingredients into a high-power mixer and process thoroughly.
2. Through a strainer, strain the juice and transfer into four glasses.
3. Enjoy immediately.

Protein Smoothie

Servings|2   Time|10 minutes
Nutritional Content (per serving):
Cal| 198   Fat| 8.4g   Protein| 24.5g   Carbs| 5.4g   Fibre| 1.6g

Ingredients:

- ❖ 2 scoops egg protein powder
- ❖ 10 millilitres (2 teaspoons) organic vanilla extract
- ❖ 4-6 ice cubes
- ❖ 15 grams (1 tablespoon) almond butter
- ❖ 6-8 drops liquid stevia
- ❖ 360 millilitres (1½ cups) unsweetened almond milk

Directions:

1. Put protein powder and remnant ingredients into a high-power mixer and process to form a creamy smoothie.
2. Put the smoothie into two glasses and enjoy immediately.

Coffee Banana Smoothie

Servings|2   Time|10 minutes
Nutritional Content (per serving):
Cal| 132   Fat| 2.5g   Protein| 14g   Carbs| 14.5g   Fibre| 2g

Ingredients:

- ❖ 1 large-sized frozen unripe banana, peel removed and slivered
- ❖ 1 scoop unflavored whey protein powder
- ❖ 240 millilitres (1 cup) cold brewed coffee

Directions:

1. Put banana and remnant ingredients into a high-power mixer and process to form a creamy smoothie.
2. Put the smoothie into two glasses and enjoy immediately.

Raspberry Tofu Smoothie

Servings | 2   Time | 10 minutes
Nutritional Content (per serving):
Cal | 82   Fat | 4.2g   Protein | 3.8g   Carbs | 9.3g   Fibre | 4.1g

Ingredients:

- 55 grams (2 ounces) firm tofu, pressed and drained
- 360 millilitres (1½ cups) unsweetened almond milk
- 125 grams (1 cup) frozen raspberries
- 2-3 drops liquid stevia
- 4-6 ice cubes

Directions:

1. Put tofu and remnant ingredients into a high-power mixer and process to form a creamy smoothie.
2. Put the smoothie into two glasses and enjoy immediately.

Strawberry Smoothie

Servings | 2   Time | 10 minutes
Nutritional Content (per serving):
Cal | 131   Fat | 3.7g   Protein | 1.6g   Carbs | 25.3g   Fibre | 4.8g

Ingredients:

- 190 grams (1½ cups) frozen strawberries
- 1¼ millilitres (¼ teaspoon) organic vanilla extract
- 1 banana, peel removed and slivered
- 480 millilitres (2 cups) chilled unsweetened almond milk

Directions:

1. Put strawberries and remnant ingredients into a high-power mixer and process to form a creamy smoothie.
2. Put the smoothie into two glasses and enjoy immediately.

Papaya Smoothie

Servings | 2   Time | 10 minutes
Nutritional Content (per serving):
Cal | 114   Fat | 3g   Protein | 1.7g   Carbs | 22.9g   Fibre | 3.5g

Ingredients:

- ❖ 145 grams (1 cup) papaya, peel removed and roughly cut up
- ❖ 360 millilitres (1½ cups) unsweetened almond milk
- ❖ 1 unripe banana, peel removed and slivered
- ❖ 15 millilitres (1 tablespoon) fresh lime juice
- ❖ 4-6 ice cubes

Directions:

1. Put papaya and remnant ingredients into a high-power mixer and process to form a creamy smoothie.
2. Put the smoothie into two glasses and enjoy immediately.

Matcha Smoothie

Servings | 2   Time | 10 minutes
Nutritional Content (per serving):
Cal | 85   Fat | 5.5g   Protein | 4g   Carbs | 7.6g   Fibre | 4.1g   Protein | 4g

Ingredients:

- ❖ 20 grams (2 tablespoons) chia seeds
- ❖ 2½ millilitres (½ teaspoon) fresh lemon juice
- ❖ 360 millilitres (1½ cups) unsweetened almond milk
- ❖ 10 grams (2 teaspoons) matcha green tea powder
- ❖ 10 drops liquid stevia
- ❖ 65 grams (¼ cup) lactose-free yoghurt
- ❖ 4-6 ice cubes

Directions:

1. Put chia seeds and remnant ingredients into a high-power mixer and process to form a creamy smoothie.
2. Put the smoothie into two glasses and enjoy immediately.

Spinach & Lettuce Smoothie

Servings | 2   Time | 10 minutes
Nutritional Content (per serving):
Cal | 23   Fat | 0.4g   Protein | 1.6g   Carbs | 4g   Fibre | 1.9g

Ingredients:

- 150 grams (2 cups) romaine lettuce, cut up
- 10 grams (¼ cup) fresh mint leaves
- 8-10 drops liquid stevia
- 8-10 drops liquid stevia
- 4-6 ice cubes
- 60 grams(2 cups) fresh baby spinach
- 30 millilitres (2 tablespoons) fresh lemon juice
- 360 millilitres (1½ cups) water

Directions:

1. Put lettuce and remnant ingredients into a high-power mixer and process to form a creamy smoothie.
2. Put the smoothie into two glasses and enjoy immediately.

Kale & Celery Smoothie

Servings | 2   Time | 10 minutes
Nutritional Content (per serving):
Cal | 65   Fat | 2.7g   Protein | 2.8g   Carbs | 8.8g   Fibre | 1.9g

Ingredients:

- 1110 grams (2 cups) fresh kale, tough ribs removed and cut up
- 360 millilitres (1½ cups) unsweetened almond milk
- 1 celery stalk, cut up
- 5 grams (½ teaspoon) fresh ginger, cut up
- 4-6 ice cubes

Directions:

1. Put kale and remnant ingredients into a high-power mixer and process to form a creamy smoothie.
2. Put the smoothie into two glasses and enjoy immediately.

Cucumber & Parsley Smoothie

Servings | 2   Time | 10 minutes
Nutritional Content (per serving):
Cal | 44   Fat | 0.8g   Protein | 2.7g   Carbs | 8.5g   Fibre | 2.7g

Ingredients:

- 240 grams (2 cups) cucumber, peel removed and cut up
- 30 millilitres (2 tablespoons) fresh lemon juice
- 480 millilitres (2 cups) chilled water
- 50 grams (2 cups) fresh parsley
- 5 grams (1 teaspoon) fresh ginger, peel removed and cut up
- 4-6 drops liquid stevia

Directions:

1. Put cucumber and remnant ingredients into a high-power mixer and process to form a creamy smoothie.
2. Put the smoothie into two glasses and enjoy immediately.

Green Veggies Smoothie

Servings | 2   Time | 10 minutes
Nutritional Content (per serving):
Cal | 19   Fat | 0.2g   Protein | 1.2g   Carbs | 4.1g   Fibre | 1.3g

Ingredients:

- 30 grams (1 cup) fresh spinach
- 25 grams (¼ cup) green cabbage, cut up
- 8-10 drops liquid stevia
- 480 millilitres (2 cups) chilled water
- 25 grams (¼ cup) broccoli florets, cut up
- ½ of small green capsicum, seeds removed and cut up

Directions:

1. Put spinach and remnant ingredients into a high-power mixer and process to form a creamy smoothie.
2. Put the smoothie into two glasses and enjoy immediately.

Breakfast Recipes

Acai Smoothie Bowl

Servings | 2   Time | 10 minutes
Nutritional Content (per serving):
Cal | 103   Fat | 8.4g   Protein | 4.5g   Carbs | 9.3g   Fibre | 7.2g

Ingredients:

- 1 packet frozen acai berry puree
- 65 grams (½ cup) fresh strawberries
- 75 grams (½ cup) fresh blueberries
- 1 scoop egg protein powder
- 2 frozen unripe bananas, peel removed and cut into chunks
- 15 grams (1 tablespoon) natural peanut butter

Directions:

1. Put acai berry puree and remnant ingredients into a high-power processor and process to form a smooth mixture.
2. Enjoy immediately with your desired topping.

Strawberry Smoothie Bowl

Servings | 2   Time | 10 minutes
Nutritional Content (per serving):
Cal | 83   Fat | 1.5g   Protein | 5.4g   Carbs | 13.7g   Fibre | 3.1g

Ingredients:

- 250 grams (2 cups) frozen strawberries
- 65 grams (¼ cup) lactose-free yoghurt
- ½ scoop whey protein powder
- 120 millilitres (½ cup) unsweetened almond milk
- 2-3 drops liquid stevia

Directions:

1. Put frozen strawberries into a high-powdered mixer and process for around 1 minute.
2. Put the almond milk, yoghurt and protein powder and process to form a smooth mixture.
3. Enjoy immediately with your desired topping.

Cheese & Yoghurt Bowl

Servings | 2   Time | 10 minutes
Nutritional Content (per serving):
Cal | 244   Fat | 16.2g   Protein | 18.5g   Carbs | 33.7g   Fibre | 6.7g

Ingredients:

- 190 grams (¾ cup) lactose-free yoghurt
- 10 millilitres (2 teaspoons) olive oil
- 70 grams (½ cup) fresh blackberries
- 30 grams (¼ cup) fresh raspberries
- 30 grams (¼ cup) gluten-free granola
- 80 grams (½ cup) cottage cheese
- 1¼ grams (¼ teaspoon) ground cinnamon
- 40 grams (¼ cup) fresh blueberries
- 15 grams (2 tablespoons) unsweetened coconut, shredded

Directions:

1. Put the yoghurt, cheese, oil and cinnamon into a large-sized bowl and blend to incorporate thoroughly.
2. Divide the yoghurt mixture in two serving bowls.
3. Top with berries, granola and coconut and enjoy immediately.

Strawberry Chia Pudding

Servings | 4   Time | 10 minutes
Nutritional Content (per serving):
Cal | 116   Fat | 5.7g   Protein | 3.5g   Carbs | 19.6g   Fibre | 6.1g

Ingredients:

- 160 millilitres (2/3 cup) unsweetened almond milk
- 250 grams (2 cups) frozen strawberries
- 1 frozen unripe banana, peel removed and slivered
- 80 grams (½ cup) chia seeds

Directions:

1. Put almond milk and remnant ingredients into a food processor except for chia seeds and process to form a smooth mixture.
2. Transfer the milk mixture into a bowl.
3. Put in chia seeds and blend to incorporate thoroughly.
4. Refrigerate for 30 minutes, blending after every 5 minutes.

Blueberry Oatmeal

Servings|2 Time|20 minutes
Nutritional Content (per serving):
Cal| 259   Fat| 6.3g   Protein| 6.6g   Carbs| 45.9g   Fibre| 5.6g

Ingredients:

- 480 millilitres (2 cups) unsweetened almond milk
- 15 millilitres (1 tablespoon) fresh lemon juice
- 100 grams (1 cup) gluten-free oats
- 40 grams (¼ cup) frozen blueberries
- 40 grams (2 tablespoons) pure maple syrup

Directions:

1. Put the almond milk, oats and blueberries into a saucepan on burner at around medium heat.
2. Cook for around 8-10 minutes.
3. Take off the pan of oatmeal from burner and blend in the maple syrup and lemon juice.
4. Enjoy moderately hot.

Oatmeal Yoghurt Bowl

Servings|2 Time|20 minutes
Nutritional Content (per serving):
Cal| 239   Fat| 3g   Protein| 6.7g   Carbs| 46.8g   Fibre| 4g

Ingredients:

- 480 millilitres (2 cups) water
- 115 grams (4 ounces) lactose-free yoghurt
- 40 grams (2 tablespoons) pure maple syrup
- 100 grams (1 cup) gluten-free old-fashioned oats

Directions:

1. Put water into a saucepan on burner at around medium heat.
2. Cook the water until boiling.
3. Blend in the oats.   Cook about 5 minutes, blending from time to time.
4. Take off the pan of oats from burner and blend in yoghurt and maple syrup.
5. Enjoy moderately hot.

Overnight Seeds Porridge

Servings | 2   Time | 10 minutes
Nutritional Content (per serving):
Cal | 202   Fat | 16.5g   Protein | 10.8g   Carbs | 4.4g   Fibre | 2.6g

Ingredients:

- 220 millilitres (2/3 cup plus ¼ cup) unsweetened coconut milk, divided
- 3-4 drops liquid stevia
- 1 pinch of salt
- 80 grams (½ cup) hemp hearts
- 10 grams (1 tablespoon) chia seeds
- 2½ millilitres (½ teaspoon) organic vanilla extract

Directions:

1. Put 160 millilitres (2/3 cup) of the coconut milk, hemp hearts, chia seed, stevia, vanilla extract and salt into a large-sized airtight container and blend to incorporate thoroughly.
2. Cover the container tightly and refrigerate overnight
3. Just before serving Put the remnant coconut milk and blend to incorporate.
4. Enjoy immediately.

Quinoa Porridge

Servings | 4   Time | 40 minutes
Nutritional Content (per serving):
Cal | 283   Fat | 11.7g   Protein | 7g   Carbs | 36g   Fibre | 3.1g

Ingredients:

- 190 grams (1 cup) uncooked quinoa, rinsed
- 240 millilitres 240 millilitres (1 cup) unsweetened coconut milk
- 1 pinch of salt
- 240 millilitres (1 cup) unsweetened almond milk
- 40 grams (2 tablespoons) pure maple syrup

Directions:

1. Sizzle an anti-sticking saucepan on burner at around medium heat.
2. Cook the quinoa for around 3 minutes, blending frequently
3. Put the almond milk, coconut milk and a 1 pinch of salt and blend to incorporate
4. Immediately turn the heat at around high.
5. Cook the mixture until boiling.
6. Immediately turn the heat at around low.
7. Cook for around 20-25 minutes, blending from time to time.
8. Take off the saucepan of quinoa from burner and immediately blend in the maple syrup.
9. Enjoy moderately hot.

Buckwheat Porridge

Servings | 3   Time | 25 minutes
Nutritional Content (per serving):
Cal | 145   Fat | 2.3g   Protein | 2.8g   Carbs | 30.5g   Fibre | 3.2g

Ingredients:

- 360 millilitres (1½ cups) water
- 2½ millilitres (½ teaspoon) organic vanilla extract
- 40 grams (2 tablespoons) pure maple syrup
- 1 unripe banana, peel removed and mashed
- 180 grams (1 cup) buckwheat groats, rinsed
- 2½ grams (½ teaspoon) ground cinnamon
- 1¼ grams (¼ teaspoon) salt
- 360 millilitres (1½ cups) unsweetened almond milk

Directions:

1. Put the water, buckwheat, vanilla extract, cinnamon and salt into a Dutch oven on burner at around medium-high heat.
2. Cook the mixture until boiling.
3. Immediately turn the heat at around medium-low.
4. Cook for around 6 minutes, blending from time to time.
5. Put in maple syrup, banana and almond milk.
6. Cook with the cover for around 6 minutes.
7. Enjoy moderately hot.

Bulgur Porridge

Servings | 2   Time | 25 minutes
Nutritional Content (per serving):
Cal | 173   Fat | 1.7g   Protein | 4.3g   Carbs | 35.5g   Fibre | 4.9g

Ingredients:

- ❖ 160 millilitres (2/3 cup) unsweetened almond milk
- ❖ 1 pinch of salt
- ❖ 70 grams (1/3 cup) bulgur, rinsed
- ❖ 1 medium-sized unripe banana, peel removed and mashed

Directions:

1. Put the almond milk, bulgur and salt into a medium-sized saucepan on burner at around medium-high heat.
2. Cook the mixture until boiling.
3. Immediately turn the heat at around low.
4. Cook for around 10 minutes.
5. Take off the pan of bulgur from burner and immediately blend in the mashed banana.
6. Enjoy moderately hot

Maple Pancakes

Servings | 5   Time | 25 minutes
Nutritional Content (per serving):
Cal | 182   Fat | 5.7g   Protein | 4.5g   Carbs | 29.3g   Fibre | 5.8g

Ingredients:

- ❖ 240 millilitres (1 cup) unsweetened coconut milk
- ❖ 15 grams (2 tablespoons) ground flaxseeds
- ❖ 1¼ grams (¼ teaspoon) salt
- ❖ 5 millilitres (1 teaspoon) organic vanilla extract
- ❖ 10 millilitres (2 teaspoons) apple cider vinegar

- ❖ 125 grams (1 cup) buckwheat flour
- ❖ 12 grams (1 tablespoon) baking powder
- ❖ 80 grams (¼ cup) maple syrup
- ❖ 15 millilitres 15 millilitres (1 tablespoon) olive oil

Directions:

1. Put the coconut milk and vinegar into a medium-sized bowl and blend to incorporate. Set aside.
2. Put the flour, flaxseeds, baking powder and salt into a large-sized bowl and blend to incorporate.
3. Put in coconut milk mixture, maple syrup and vanilla extract and whisk to incorporate thoroughly.
4. Sizzle oil into a large-sized anti-sticking wok on burner at around medium heat.
5. Place desired amount of the mixture and spread into an even circle.
6. Cook for around 1-2 minutes
7. Change the side of pancake and cook for around 1 minute.
8. Repeat with the remnant mixture.
9. Enjoy moderately hot.

Banana Waffles

Servings | 5   Time | 30 minutes
Nutritional Content (per serving):
Cal | 376   Fat | 30.5g   Protein | 8.6g   Carbs | 22.3g   Fibre | 3.9g

Ingredients:

- 15 grams (2 tablespoons) flaxseeds meal
- 2 unripe bananas, peel removed and mashed
- 60 millilitres (¼ cup) unsweetened coconut milk
- 90 millilitres (6 tablespoons) warm water
- 240 grams (1 cup) creamy almond butter
- Olive oil baking spray

Directions:

1. Put the flaxseed meal and warm water into a small-sized bowl and whisk to incorporate thoroughly.
2. Set aside for around 10 minutes.
3. Put the bananas, almond butter and coconut milk into a medium-sized mixing bowl and blend to incorporate thoroughly.
4. Put the flaxseed meal mixture and blend to incorporate thoroughly.
5. Preheat your waffle iron and then lightly spray it with baking spray.
6. Place desired amount of the mixture in the preheated waffle iron.
7. Cook for around 3-4 minutes.
8. Repeat with the remnant mixture.
9. Enjoy moderately hot.

Blueberry Muffins

Servings | 8   Time | 35 minutes
Nutritional Content (per serving):
Cal | 57   Fat | 1.9g   Protein | 2.3g   Carbs | 8 g   Fibre | 1.7g

Ingredients:

- Olive oil baking spray
- 50 grams (½ cup) gluten-free rolled oats
- 20 grams (2 tablespoons) flaxseeds
- 2½ grams (½ teaspoon) ground cinnamon
- 1 egg
- 30 grams (¼ cup) buckwheat flour
- 2 grams (½ teaspoon) baking soda
- 90 grams (¼ cup) almond butter
- 30 grams (2 tablespoons) unripe banana, mashed
- 40 grams (¼ cup) fresh blueberries

Directions:

1. For preheating: set your oven at 190 °C (375 °F).
2. Lightly spray 8 holes of a muffin pan with baking spray.
3. Put oats and remnant ingredients except the blueberries into a clean mixer and process to form a smooth mixture.
4. Put the blended mixture into a bowl and Lightly blend in blueberries.
5. Put the blended mixture into the muffin holes.
6. Bake in your oven for around 10-12 minutes.
7. Take off the muffin tin from oven and place onto a metal rack to cool for around 10 minutes.
8. Then invert the muffins onto the metal rack to cool before enjoying it.

Courgette Bread

Servings | 8   Time | 1 hour
Nutritional Content (per serving):
Cal | 229   Fat | 14.9g   Protein | 3.7g   Carbs | 23.1g   Fibre | 2.5g

Ingredients:

- 190 grams (1½ cups) buckwheat flour
- 5 grams (1 teaspoon) ground cinnamon
- 1 egg
- 5 grams (1 tablespoon) lemon zest, grated
- 60 grams (½ cup) courgette, shredded

- 4 grams (1 teaspoon) baking soda
- 2½ grams (½ teaspoon) salt
- 80 grams (¼ cup) maple syrup
- 100 grams (½ cup) coconut oil

Directions:

1. For preheating: set your oven at 175 °C (350 °F).
2. Line a bread pan with bakery paper.
3. Put the flour, baking soda, cinnamon powderand salt into a large-sized bowl and blend to incorporate.   .
4. Put egg, maple syrup, lemon zest and oil into another medium-sized bowl and with an electric mixer, whisk to incorporate thoroughly
5. Put egg mixture in the bowl of flour mixture and blend until just incorporated.
6. Lightly blend in the courgette.
7. Put the mixture into the loaf pan.
8. Bake in your oven for around 45 minutes.
9. Take off the loaf pan from oven and place onto a metal rack to cool for around 10 minutes.
10. Then invert the bread onto the metal rack to cool thoroughly.
11. Cut the bread loaf into serving portions and enjoy.

Oats & Quinoa Granola

Servings | 12   Time | 40 minutes
Nutritional Content (per serving):
Cal | 115   Fat | 6.4g   Protein | 3.5g   Carbs | 12.5g   Fibre | 2.5g

Ingredients:

- 100 grams (1 cup) quick-cooking steel-cut oats
- 60 grams (½ cup) walnuts, roughly cut up
- ¾ gram (1/8 teaspoon) salt
- 45 millilitres (3 tablespoons) olive oil
- 25 grams (¼ cup) unsweetened coconut flakes
- 95 grams (½ cup) uncooked quinoa, rinsed
- 40 grams (¼ cup) chia seeds
- 60 grams (3 tablespoons) pure maple syrup
- 5 millilitres (1 teaspoon) organic vanilla extract

Directions:

1. For preheating: set your oven at 165 °C (325 °F).
2. Arrange a rack on a third rack from the bottom of oven.
3. Line a baking tray with bakery paper.
4. Put oats, quinoa, walnuts, chia seeds and salt into a medium-sized bowl.
5. Put in maple syrup, oil and vanilla extract and blend to incorporate thoroughly
6. Transfer the oat mixture onto the baking tray and spread into an even layer.
7. Bake in your oven for around 25 minutes.
8. Sprinkle the top of the granola with coconut flakes and bake in your oven for around 5 minutes more.
9. Take off from oven and set aside to cool thoroughly.
10. Break the granola into pieces and enjoy with your favorite milk and topping.

Tomato & Egg Scramble

Servings|2   Time|15 minutes
Nutritional Content (per serving):
Cal| 195   Fat| 15.9g   Protein| 11.6g   Carbs| 2.6g   Fibre| 0.7g

Ingredients:

- 4 eggs
- Salt and ground black pepper, as required
- 100 grams (½ cup) tomatoes, cut up
- 1¼ grams (¼ teaspoon) red pepper flakes
- 10 grams (¼ cup) fresh basil, cut up
- 15 millilitres (1 tablespoon) olive oil

Directions:

1. Put eggs, red pepper flakes, salt and pepper into a large-sized bowl and whisk thoroughly.
2. Put in basil and tomatoes and blend to incorporate.
3. Sizzle oil into a large-sized anti-sticking wok on burner at around medium-high heat.
4. Put in egg mixture and cook for around 3-5 minutes, blending continuously.
5. Enjoy immediately.

Salmon Omelet

Servings | 2   Time | 15 minutes
Nutritional Content (per serving):
Cal | 309   Fat | 24.9g   Protein | 20.8g   Carbs | 1.1g   Fibre | 0g

Ingredients:

- ❖ 4 eggs
- ❖ 25 grams (2 tablespoons) coconut oil
- ❖ 15 grams (2 tablespoons) feta cheese, crumbled
- ❖ Salt and ground black pepper, as required
- ❖ 85 grams (3 ounces) cooked salmon, roughly cut up

Directions:

1. Into a bowl and gently whisk to incorporate thoroughly.
2. Sizzle oil into a frying pan on burner at around medium heat.
3. Put in whisked eggs and cook for around 1-2 minutes, without mixing.
4. Carefully lift the edges to run the
5. Put the salmon pieces into the center of the omelet.
6. Cook for around 40-50 seconds.
7. Top with cheese and cook for around 20-40 seconds.
8. Take off from burner and put the omelet onto a plate.
9. Enjoy immediately.

Green Veggies Quiche

Servings | 4   Time | 35 minutes
Nutritional Content (per serving):
Cal | 176   Fat | 10.9g   Protein | 15.4g   Carbs | 5g   Fibre | 0.9g

Ingredients:

- Olive oil baking spray
- 120 millilitres (½ cup) unsweetened almond milk
- 75 grams (½ cup) green capsicum, seeds removed and cut up
- 20 grams (3 tablespoons) mozzarella cheese, grated
- 6 eggs
- Salt and ground black pepper, as required
- 60 grams (2 cups) fresh spinach, cut up
- 25 grams 25 grams (¼ cup) green onion, cut up
- 10 grams (¼ cup) fresh coriander, cut up
- 5 grams (1 tablespoon) fresh chives, finely cut up

Directions:

1. For preheating: set your oven at 205 °C (400 °F).
2. Lightly spray a pie dish with baking spray.
3. Put eggs, almond milk, salt and pepper into a bowl and whisk to incorporate thoroughly. Set aside.
4. Put the vegetables and herbs into another bowl and blend to incorporate thoroughly.
5. Put the veggie mixture into the pie dish and top with the egg mixture.
6. Bake in your oven for around 20 minutes.
7. Take off the pie dish from oven and immediately sprinkle with the mozzarella cheese.
8. Set aside for around 5 minutes before slicing.
9. Cut into serving portions and enjoy moderately hot.

Chicken & Veggies Frittata

Servings | 6   Time | 1 hour
Nutritional Content (per serving):
Cal | 223   Fat | 12g   Protein | 24.9g   Carbs | 3.5g   Fibre | 0.9g

Ingredients:

- ❖ Olive oil baking spray
- ❖ 50 grams 50 grams (½ cup) green onion, slivered
- ❖ 150 grams (1 cup) capsicum, seeds removed and cut up
- ❖ 4 large-sized egg whites
- ❖ 110 grams (1 cup) cheddar cheese, shredded
- ❖ 10 grams (1 tablespoon) Parmesan cheese, shredded

- ❖ 5 millilitres (1 teaspoon) olive oil
- ❖ 60 grams (2 cups) fresh spinach, cut up
- ❖ 280 grams (2 cups) cooked chicken, cut up
- ❖ 3 large-sized eggs
- ❖ 300 millilitres (1¼ cups) unsweetened almond milk
- ❖ Salt and ground black pepper, as required

Directions:

1. For preheating: set your oven at 175 °C (350 °F).
2. Spray a 9-inch pie plate with baking spray.
3. Sizzle oil into a wok on burner at around medium heat.
4. Cook the green onion for around 2-3 minutes
5. Blend in the spinach and capsicum and cook for around 1-2 minutes.
6. Blend in chicken and transfer the mixture into the pie dish.
7. Add eggs, egg whites, almond milk, cheddar cheese, salt and pepper into a bowl and whisk to incorporate thoroughly.
8. Pour egg mixture over the chicken mixture and top with Parmesan cheese.
9. Bake in your oven for around 40 minutes.
10. Take off the pie dish from oven and set aside for around 5 minutes.
11. Cut into serving portions and enjoy.

Eggs with Beef & Tomatoes

Servings | 4   Time | 55 minutes
Nutritional Content (per serving):
Cal | 378   Fat | 24.9g   Protein | 27.6g   Carbs | 15.4g   Fibre | 5 g

Ingredients:

- 45 millilitres (3 tablespoons) olive oil
- 2 capsicums, seeds removed and cut up
- 10 grams (¼ cup) fresh coriander, cut up and divided
- 10 grams (2 teaspoons) paprika
- 155 grams (2 ounces) lean ground beef
- 4 eggs

- 150 grams (1½ cups) green onion, cut into slices
- 5 grams (3 tablespoons) fresh parsley, cut up
- 5 grams (1 teaspoon) dried thyme
- 5 grams (1 teaspoon) ground cumin
- 2 (400-gram) (14-ounce) cans diced tomatoes
- 55 grams (2 ounces) feta cheese, crumbled

Directions:

1. Sizzle oil into a large-sized shallow, flat-bottomed wok on burner and heat at around medium heat.
2. Cook the green onion for around 2-3 minutes.
3. Put in the capsicums and cook for around 5 minutes, blending regularly.
4. Put in half of coriander, parsley, thyme, paprika and cumin.
5. Cook for around 2 minutes, blending regularly.
6. Put in the ground beef and cook for around 4-5 minutes, blending regularly
7. Put in the tomatoes, salt and pepper.
8. Cook for around 15-20 minutes, blending from time to time.
9. With a spoon, make 4 wells in the greens mixture.
10. Carefully crack 1 egg into each well and sprinkle each egg with a bit of salt.
11. Cook with the cover for around 5 minutes
12. Take off from burner and enjoy hot with the garnishing of remnant coriander.

Lunch Recipes

Egg Salad

Servings | 2   Time | 10 minutes
Nutritional Content (per serving):
Cal | 211   Fat | 14.1g   Protein | 13g   Carbs | 8.4g   Fibre | 0.7g

Ingredients:

- ❖ 4 hard-boiled eggs, peel removed and cut up
- ❖ 65 grams (¼ cup) lactose-free yoghurt
- ❖ Salt and ground black pepper, as required
- ❖ 25 grams (¼ cup) green onion, cut up
- ❖ 20 grams (2 tablespoons) mayonnaise
- ❖ 150 grams (2 cups) lettuce, torn

Directions:

1. Put egg pieces, green onion, yoghurt, mayonnaise, salt and pepper into a medium-sized salad bowl and gently blend to incorporate.
2. Line a serving plate with lettuce
3. Top with egg mixture and enjoy immediately.

Raspberry Salad

Servings | 2   Time | 10 minutes
Nutritional Content (per serving):
Cal | 163   Fat | 11.8g   Protein | 4.3g   Carbs | 12.6g   Fibre | 3.5g

Ingredients:

For Salad:

- ❖ 110 grams (2 cups) fresh baby kale
- ❖ 65 grams (½ cup) fresh raspberries
- ❖ 15 grams (2 tablespoons) walnuts, toasted and cut up

For Dressing:

- ❖ 15 millilitres (1 tablespoon) olive oil
- ❖ 15 millilitres (1 tablespoon) apple cider vinegar
- ❖ 5 grams (1 teaspoon) pure maple syrup
- ❖ Salt and ground black pepper, as required

Directions:

1. For the salad: put kale and remnant ingredients into a salad bowl and blend.
2. For the dressing: put oil and remnant ingredients into another bowl and whisk to incorporate thoroughly.
3. Place dressing on top of salad and toss to incorporate thoroughly.
4. Enjoy immediately.

Courgette & Tomato Salad

Servings | 4   Time | 15 minutes
Nutritional Content (per serving):
Cal | 93   Fat | 7.4g   Protein | 2g   Carbs | 6.9g   Fibre | 2.2g

Ingredients:

- ❖ 2 medium-sized courgettes, slivered thinly
- ❖ 30 millilitres (2 tablespoons) olive oil
- ❖ 1 pinch of salt
- ❖ 400 grams (2 cups) tomatoes, slivered
- ❖ 30 millilitres (2 tablespoons) fresh lime juice

Directions:

1. Into a salad bowl Put all ingredients and gently toss to combine.
2. Enjoy immediately.

Veggie Lettuce Wraps

Servings | 3   Time | 15 minutes
Nutritional Content (per serving):
Cal | 30   Fat | 0.2g   Protein | 0.9g   Carbs | 7.1g   Fibre | 1.6g

Ingredients:

- ❖ 150 grams (1 cup) multi-colored capsicums, seeds removed and Julienned
- ❖ 10 grams (¼ cup) fresh chives
- ❖ 6 large-sized lettuce leaves
- ❖ 150 grams (1 cup) carrots, peel removed and slivered
- ❖ Salt, as required

Directions:

1. Put the capsicum, carrot chives and salt into a large-sized bowl and blend thoroughly.
2. Arrange the lettuce leaves onto serving plates.
3. Top each leaf with kale mixture and enjoy immediately.

Chicken Lettuce Wraps

Servings|2   Time|15 minutes
Nutritional Content (per serving):
Cal| 131   Fat| 2.2g   Protein| 21.2g   Carbs| 5.9g   Fibre| 1.4g

Ingredients:

- ❖ 140 grams (1 cup) cooked chicken, cut up
- ❖ Salt and ground black pepper, as required
- ❖ 75 grams (½ cup) carrot, peel removed and julienned

- ❖ 35-45 grams (4-5 tablespoons) tomato puree
- ❖ 4 large-sized lettuce leaves
- ❖ 5 grams (1 tablespoon) fresh parsley, cut up

Directions:

1. Into a bowl Put chicken, tomato puree, salt and pepper and blend to incorporate thoroughly
2. Arrange the lettuce leaves onto serving plates.
3. Put the chicken mixture over each lettuce leaf and top with carrot and parsley.
4. Enjoy immediately.

Beef Burgers

Servings|4   Time|30 minutes
Nutritional Content (per serving):
Cal| 225   Fat| 17.6g   Protein| 14.1g   Carbs| 3g   Fibre| 0.7g

Ingredients:

- ❖ 455 grams (1 pound) ground beef
- ❖ 30 grams (¼ cup) sun-dried tomatoes, cut up
- ❖ 1 egg, whisked
- ❖ Salt and ground black pepper, as required
- ❖ 300 grams (4 cups) lettuce, torn
- ❖ 145 grams (1½ cups) fresh baby spinach leaves, cut up
- ❖ 30 grams (¼ cup) feta cheese, crumbled
- ❖ 30 grams (2 tablespoons) unsalted butter

Directions:

1. For burgers: put ground beef and remnant ingredients except for butter and lettuce into a large-sized bowl and blend to incorporate thoroughly.
2. Make 4 equal-sized patties from the mixture.
3. Sizzle butter into a cast-iron wok on burner at around medium-high heat.
4. Cook the patties for around 5-6 minutes per side.
5. Divide the lettuce onto serving plates and top each with 1 burger.
6. Enjoy immediately.

Turkey Meatballs

Servings | 8   Time | 30 minutes
Nutritional Content (per serving):
Cal | 231   Fat | 12.7g   Protein | 19.7g   Carbs | 13.2g   Fibre | 3.3g

Ingredients:

- 455 grams (1 pound) ground turkey
- 2 small-sized capsicums, seeds removed and finely cut up
- Salt and ground black pepper, as required
- 440 grams (8 cups) fresh baby kale
- 170 grams (1 cup) cooked black beans, mashed roughly
- 10 grams (½ cup) fresh parsley, cut up
- 60 millilitres (¼ cup) olive oil

Directions:

1. Put ground turkey and remnant ingredients except for oil and kale into a large-sized bowl and blend to incorporate thoroughly.
2. Make equal-sized balls from the mixture.
3. Sizzle oil into a large-sized anti-sticking wok on burner at around medium heat.
4. Cook the meatballs for around 5-7 minutes.
5. Cover the wok and cook for around 5 minutes.
6. Enjoy hot alongside the kale.

Egg Drop Soup

Servings | 6   Time | 30 minutes
Nutritional Content (per serving):
Cal | 92   Fat | 5.3g   Protein | 7 g   Carbs | 3.4g   Fibre | 0.2g

Ingredients:

- 15 millilitres (1 tablespoon) olive oil
- 1440 millilitres (6 cups) low-FODMAP chicken broth, divided
- 90 millilitres (1/3 cup) fresh lemon juice
- Ground white pepper, as required
- 5 grams (1 tablespoon) garlic, finely cut up
- 2 organic eggs
- 15 grams (1 tablespoon) arrow powder
- 25 grams (¼ cup) green onion (green part), cut up

Directions:

1. Sizzle oil into a large-sized soup pan on burner and heat at around medium-high heat.
2. Cook the garlic for around 1 minute.
3. Put in 5½ cups of broth and immediately turn the heat at around high.
4. Cook the mixture until boiling.
5. Immediately turn the heat at around medium.
6. Cook for around 5 minutes.
7. Meanwhile, put eggs, arrow powder, lemon juice, white pepper and remnant broth into a bowl and whisk to incorporate thoroughly.
8. Slowly put the egg mixture into the pan, blending regularly.
9. Cook for around 5-6 minutes, blending regularly
10. Enjoy hot with the garnishing of green onion.

Tomato Soup

Servings | 4   Time | 30 minutes
Nutritional Content (per serving):
Cal | 90   Fat | 7.3g   Protein | 1.3g   Carbs | 6.8g   Fibre | 1.9g

Ingredients:

- 30 millilitres (2 tablespoons) olive oil
- 500 grams (2½ cups) tomatoes, finely cut up
- 720 millilitres (3 cups) water
- Salt and ground black pepper, as required

- 50 grams (½ cup) green onion, cut up
- 2½ grams (½ teaspoon) dried thyme
- 5 grams (¼ cup) fresh basil leaves, cut up

Directions:

1. Sizzle oil into a large-sized soup pan on burner at around medium heat.
2. Cook the green onion for around 4-5 minutes.
3. Put the tomatoes, thyme and water.
4. Cook the mixture until boiling
5. Immediately turn the heat at around low.
6. Cook with the cover for around 15 minutes
7. Take off from burner and set aside to cool slightly.
8. Put soup into a mixer in batches and process to form a smooth mixture.
9. Return the soup in the same pan on burner at around medium heat.
10. Blend in basil and cook for around 3-4 minutes.
11. Blend in salt and pepper and enjoy hot.

Stuffed Capsicums

Servings|4   Time|35 minutes
Nutritional Content (per serving):
Cal| 264   Fat| 16.3g   Protein| 16.5g   Carbs| 15.5g   Fibre| 3.4g

Ingredients:

- 10 millilitres (2 teaspoons) olive oil
- 100 grams (1 cup) fresh oyster mushrooms, cut up
- 100 grams (½ cup) tomato puree
- 115 grams (4 ounces) sharp cheddar cheese, shredded
- 455 grams (1 pound) lean ground beef
- 150 grams (1½ cups) green onion, cut up
- Salt and ground black pepper, as required
- 4 large-sized capsicums, halved lengthwise and cored
- 240 millilitres (1 cup) water

Directions:

1. Sizzle oil into a flat-bottomed wok at around medium-high heat.
2. Cook the beef for around 5 minutes.
3. Put in the mushrooms and green onion.
4. Cook for around 5-6 minutes.
5. Put in salt and pepper and cook for around 1 minute
6. Take off the pan of beef mixture from burner and drain off the excess grease.
7. Put in the tomato puree and blend to incorporate.
8. Meanwhile, arrange the capsicums into a large-sized microwave-safe dish, cut-side down
9. Pour the water in the baking pan.
10. With plastic wrap, cover the baking pan and microwave on high for around 4-5 minutes
11. Take off from microwave and uncover the baking pan.
12. Dain the water thoroughly.
13. Now in the baking pan, arrange the capsicums, cut-side up.
14. Stuff the capsicums with beef mixture and top with cheese.
15. Microwave on High for around 2-3 minutes,
16. Enjoy moderately hot.

Stuffed Courgette

Servings | 8   Time | 30 minutes
Nutritional Content (per serving):
Cal | 59   Fat | 3.2g   Protein | 2.9g   Carbs | 6.2g   Fibre | 0.9g

Ingredients:

- ❖ Olive oil baking spray
- ❖ 150 grams (1 cup) capsicum, seeds removed and finely cut up
- ❖ 100 grams (½ cup) tomatoes, finely cut up
- ❖ Salt and ground black pepper, as required
- ❖ 4 medium-sized courgettes, halved lengthwise
- ❖ 90 grams (½ cup) Kalamata olives, pitted and finely cut up
- ❖ 10 grams (2 teaspoons) dried oregano
- ❖ 55 grams (½ cup) feta cheese, crumbled

Directions:

1. For preheating: set your oven at 175 °C (350 °F).
2. Spray a large-sized baking tray with baking spray.
3. With a melon baller, scoop out the flesh of each courgette half. Discard the flesh.
4. Put the capsicum, olives, tomatoes, oregano, salt and pepper into a bowl and blend to incorporate.
5. Stuff each courgette half with the veggie mixture.
6. Arrange courgette halves onto the prepared baking tray and bake in your oven for around 15 minutes.
7. Now, set the oven to broiler on high.
8. Top each courgette half with feta cheese and broil for around 3 minutes.
9. Enjoy hot.

Chicken & Veggie Kabobs

Servings | 6   Time | 25 minutes
Nutritional Content (per serving):
Cal | 201   Fat | 10.6g   Protein | 22.3g   Carbs | 4.3g   Fibre | 1.1g

Ingredients:

- 30 grams (¼ cup) Parmigiano Reggiano cheese, grated
- 20 grams (1 cup) fresh basil leaves, cut up
- 570 grams (1¼ pounds) boneless chicken breast, cut into 1-inch cubes
- 24 cherry tomatoes

- 45 millilitres (3 tablespoons) olive oil
- 2 garlic cloves, finely cut up
- Salt and ground black pepper, as required
- 1 large-sized green capsicum, seeds removed and cubed

Directions:

1. Put the cheese, butter, garlic, basil, salt and pepper into a clean food processor and process to form a smooth mixture.
2. Put the basil mixture into a large-sized bowl.
3. Put in the chicken cubes and blend thoroughly.
4. Cover the bowl and put in your refrigerator to marinate for at least 4-5 hours.
5. For preheating: set your grill to medium-high heat.
6. Generously spray the grill grate.
7. Thread the chicken, capsicum cubes and tomatoes onto presoaked wooden skewers.
8. Put the skewers onto the grill.
9. Cook for around 6-8 minutes, flipping from time to time.
10. Take off from the grill and place onto a platter for around 5 minutes before enjoying it.

Spiced Ground Chicken

Servings | 4   Time | 20 minutes
Nutritional Content (per serving):
Cal | 264   Fat | 8.3g   Protein | 8.5g   Carbs | 40.1g   Fibre | 5.1g

Ingredients:

- 30 millilitres (2 tablespoons) olive oil
- 5 grams (1 teaspoon) fresh ginger, finely cut up
- 1¼ grams (¼ teaspoon) ground coriander
- 570 grams (1¼ pounds) ground chicken
- Salt and ground black pepper, as required
- 5 grams (2 tablespoons) fresh coriander, cut up
- 50 grams (½ cup) green onion, cut up
- 1¼ grams (¼ teaspoon) ground cumin
- 1¼ grams (¼ teaspoon) cayenne pepper powder
- 10 millilitres (2 teaspoons) fresh lemon juice

Directions:

1. Sizzle oil into a wok on burner at around medium heat.
2. Cook the green onion, ginger and spices for around 2-3 minutes.
3. Put the ground chicken, salt and pepper and cook for around 6-7 minutes.
4. Blend in lemon juice and coriander.
5. Cook for around 1 minute.
6. Enjoy hot.

Chicken Gizzard with Cabbage

Servings | 2   Time | 25 minutes
Nutritional Content (per serving):
Cal | 190   Fat | 6.4g   Protein | 1.5g   Carbs | 3.3g   Fibre | 1g

Ingredients:

- 225 grams (½ pound) chicken gizzards, cut into small pieces
- 100 grams (1 cup) cabbage, cut into bite-sized pieces
- 15 millilitres (1 tablespoon) low-sodium soy sauce
- 5 grams (1 teaspoon) fresh ginger, peel removed
- 15 grams (1 tablespoon) unsalted butter
- 5 grams (½ teaspoon) fresh ginger, grated
- 5 millilitres (1 teaspoon) fresh lemon juice
- Ground black pepper, as required

Directions:

1. Put the chicken gizzard and ginger piece into a saucepan of water on burner at around medium-high heat.
2. Cook for around 2 minutes.
3. Drain the gizzard pieces and rinse under cold running water.
4. Sizzle butter into a wok on burner at around medium heat.
5. Stir-fry the gizzard pieces for around 3-4 minutes.
6. Put the cabbage and finely cut up ginger and stir-fry for around 5-6 minutes.
7. Blend in the soy sauce, lemon juice, salt and pepper.
8. Cook for around 1-2 minutes.
9. Enjoy hot.

Turkey Meatloaf

Servings | 10   Time | 55 minutes
Nutritional Content (per serving):
Cal | 224   Fat | 12.7g   Protein | 22.7g   Carbs | 4.6g   Fibre | 0.2g

Ingredients:

- ❖ 910 grams (2 pounds) lean ground turkey
- ❖ 110 grams (4 ounces) low-FODMAP BBQ sauce, divided
- ❖ 5 grams (1 teaspoon) ground mustard
- ❖ 165 grams (1½ cup) cheddar cheese, shredded
- ❖ 1 egg
- ❖ 5 grams (1 teaspoon) red chili powder
- ❖ Salt, as required

Directions:

1. For preheating: set your oven at 205 °C (400 °F).
2. Greased a 9x13-inch casserole dish with baking spray.
3. For meatloaf: put turkey, 110 grams of cheese, half of BBQ sauce, egg, chili powder, mustard and salt and blend to incorporate thoroughly.
4. Put the mixture into the casserole dish and press to smooth the surface.
5. Coat the top of meatloaf with remnant BBQ sauce and sprinkle with remnant cheese.
6. Bake in your oven for around 40 minutes.
7. Take off the meatloaf from oven and place onto a metal rack to cool slightly.
8. Cut the meatloaf into serving portions and enjoy moderately hot.

Shrimp with Kale

Servings | 6   Time | 22 minutes
Nutritional Content (per serving):
Cal | 210   Fat | 8.5g   Protein | 27g   Carbs | 8.6g   Fibre | 1.4g

Ingredients:

- 45 millilitres (3 tablespoons) olive oil
- 50 grams (½ cup) green onion, cut up
- 1 fresh red chili, slivered
- 90 millilitres (1/3 cup) low-FODMAP chicken broth
- 680 grams (1½ pounds) medium shrimp, peel removed and deveined
- 455 grams (1 pound) fresh kale, tough ribs removed and cut up

Directions:

1. Sizzle 15 millilitres (1 tablespoon) of the oil into a large-sized anti-sticking wok on burner at around medium-high heat.
2. Cook the shrimp for around 2 minutes per side.
3. With a slotted spoon, transfer the shrimp onto a plate.
4. Sizzle the remnant oil into the same wok on burner at around medium heat.
5. Cook the green onion and red chili for around 1-2 minutes.
6. Put the kale and broth and cook for around 4-5 minutes, blending from time to time.
7. Blend in the cooked shrimp.
8. Cook for around 1 minute.
9. Enjoy hot.

Scallops with Green Beans

Servings | 4   Time | 25 minutes
Nutritional Content (per serving):
Cal | 163   Fat | 6.7g   Protein | 19.6g   Carbs | 5.5g   Fibre | 1g

Ingredients:

- ❖ 30 millilitres (2 tablespoons) olive oil, divided
- ❖ 455 grams (1 pound) scallops, side muscles removed
- ❖ 2 capsicums, seeds removed and cut up
- ❖ 10 grams (2 teaspoons) dried parsley
- ❖ Salt and ground black pepper, as required

Directions:

1. Sizzle 15 millilitres (1 tablespoon) of oil into a large-sized wok on burner at around medium heat and stir-fry the capsicums for around 4-5 minutes.
2. With a slotted spoon, transfer the capsicums onto a plate.
3. Melt the remnant butter in the same wok and stir-fry the scallops for around 2 minutes.
4. Blend in parsley, salt and pepper and cook for around 1 minute.
5. Add in the cooked capsicums.
6. Cook for around 2-3 minutes.
7. Enjoy hot.

Banana Curry

Servings | 4   Time | 30 minutes
Nutritional Content (per serving):
Cal | 216   Fat | 9.1g   Protein | 6.2g   Carbs | 32 g   Fibre | 6.5g

Ingredients:

- 30 millilitres (2 tablespoons) olive oil
- 30 grams (2 tablespoons) curry powder
- 5 grams (1 teaspoon) ground cumin
- 5 grams (1 teaspoon) ground cinnamon
- Salt and ground black pepper, as required
- 200 grams (1 cup) tomato puree
- 3 tomatoes, finely cut up

- 100 grams (1 cup) green onion, cut up
- 5 grams (1 teaspoon) ground ginger
- 5 grams (1 teaspoon) ground turmeric
- 5 grams (1 teaspoon) red chili powder
- 165 grams (2/3 cup) lactose-free yoghurt
- 2 unripe bananas, peel removed and slivered

Directions:

1. Sizzle oil into a saucepan on burner and heat at around medium heat.
2. Cook the green onion for around 3-4 minutes.
3. Put in the curry powder and spices and cook for around 1 minute.
4. Put in the yoghurt and tomato sauce and cook the mixture until boiling.
5. Put in the bananas and cook for around 3 minutes.
6. Put in the tomatoes and cook for around 1-2 minutes.
7. Enjoy hot.

Spinach with Cottage Cheese

Servings | 8   Time | 40 minutes
Nutritional Content (per serving):
Cal | 121   Fat | 6.1g   Protein | 10.5g   Carbs | 7.4g   Fibre | 2.2g

Ingredients:

- 2 (286-gram) (10-ounce) packages frozen spinach, thawed and drained
- 455 grams (1 pound) cottage cheese, cut into ½-inch cubes
- 5 grams (1 tablespoon) garlic, finely cut up
- 40 grams (2 tablespoons) tomato puree
- 10 grams (2 teaspoons) curry powder
- 5 grams (1 teaspoons) ground coriander
- 5 grams (1 teaspoons) ground turmeric
- Salt, as required

- 360 millilitres (1½ cups) water, divided
- 60 grams (¼ cup) sour cream
- 30 grams (2 tablespoons) unsalted butter
- 10 grams (1 tablespoon) onion, finely cut up
- 5 grams (1 tablespoon) fresh ginger, finely cut up
- 10 grams (2 teaspoons) garam masala powder
- 5 grams (1 teaspoons) ground cumin
- 5 grams (1 teaspoons) red pepper flakes

Directions:

1. Put spinach, 120 millilitres (½ cup) of water and sour cream into a clean mixer and process to form a puree.
2. Put the spinach puree into a bowl and set it aside.
3. Sizzle butter into a large-sized anti-sticking, flat-bottomed wok on burner at around medium-low heat.
4. Cook the onion, garlic, ginger, tomato puree, spices and salt for around 2-3 minutes.
5. Put in the spinach puree and remnant water and blend to incorporate.
6. Immediately turn the heat at around medium.
7. Cook for around 3-5 minutes
8. Put in cottage cheese cubes and blend to incorporate.
9. Immediately turn the heat at around low.
10. Cook for around 10-15 minutes.
11. Enjoy hot.

Tofu with Broccoli

Servings | 4   Time | 40 minutes
Nutritional Content (per serving):
Cal | 284   Fat | 20.6g   Carbs | 19.6g   Fibre | 2.4g   Protein | 9.3g

Ingredients:

- 155 grams (2 ounces) firm tofu, pressed, drained and cut into 1-inch slices
- 5 grams (1 teaspoon) fresh ginger, grated
- 45 millilitres (3 tablespoons) low-sodium soy sauce
- 120 millilitres (½ cup) water
- 50 grams (1/3 cup) cornstarch, divided
- 90 millilitres (1/3 cup) olive oil
- 50 grams (½ cup) green onion, slivered thinly
- 30 millilitres (2 tablespoons) balsamic vinegar
- 20 grams (1 tablespoon) pure maple syrup
- 180 grams (2 cups) broccoli florets

Directions:

1. Put 35 grams (¼ cup) of the cornstarch into a shallow bowl.
2. Put the tofu cubes and coat with cornstarch.
3. Sizzle oil into a cast iron wok on burner at around medium heat.
4. Cook the tofu cubes for around 8-10 minutes.
5. With a slotted spoon, transfer the tofu cubes onto a plate. Set aside.
6. Put the ginger into the same wok and cook for around 1 minute.
7. Blend in the green onion and cook for around 2-3 minutes.
8. Put the soy sauce, vinegar and maple syrup and blend to incorporate.
9. Cook the mixture until boiling.
10. In the meantime, into a small-sized bowl, dissolve the remnant cornstarch in water.
11. Slowly put the cornstarch mixture into the sauce, blending continuously.
12. Blend in the cooked tofu and cook for around 1 minute.
13. Meanwhile, arrange a steamer basket into a saucepan of water.
14. Cook the mixture until boiling.
15. Immediately turn the heat at around medium-low.
16. Put the broccoli florets in the steamer basket and steam with the cover for around 5-6 minutes.
17. Drain the broccoli and transfer into the wok of tofu.
18. Blend the broccoli with tofu mixture and enjoy hot.

Dinner Recipes

Chicken Salad

Servings | 5   Time | 15 minutes
Nutritional Content (per serving):
Cal | 410   Fat | 25g   Protein | 30.2g   Carbs | 14g   Fibre | 1.4g

Ingredients:

- 455 grams (1 pound) cooked chicken, cut into bite-sized pieces
- 60 grams (½ cup) walnuts, cut up
- 15 millilitres (1 tablespoon) fresh lemon juice
- Salt and ground black pepper, as required

- 50 grams (½ cup) dried cranberries
- 300 grams (3 cups) celery stalks, cut up
- 130 grams (1 cup) mayonnaise
- 45 millilitres (3 tablespoons) balsamic vinegar

Directions:

1. Put cooked chicken and remnant ingredients into a large-sized salad bowl and blend to incorporate thoroughly.
2. Enjoy immediately.

Pork Salad

Servings|6   Time|15 minutes
Nutritional Content (per serving):
Cal| 270   Fat| 8.3g   Protein| 31.3g   Carbs| 15.9g   Fibre| 1.3g

Ingredients:

- 455 grams (1 pound) cooked pork, cut into slices
- 90 grams (3 cups) fresh baby spinach
- 20 millilitres (4 teaspoons) olive oil
- Salt and ground black pepper, as required
- 3 oranges, peel removed and sectioned
- 225 grams (3 cups) lettuce, torn
- 30 millilitres (2 tablespoons) fresh orange juice
- 3-4 drops liquid stevia

Directions:

1. Put cooked pork and remnant ingredients into a large-sized salad bowl and toss to incorporate thoroughly.
2. Enjoy immediately.

Salmon Salad

Servings|6   Time|15 minutes
Nutritional Content (per serving):
Cal| 297   Fat| 14.2g   Protein| 18.7g   Carbs| 26.5g   Fibre| 6.1g

Ingredients:

- 155 grams (2 ounces) cooked salmon, cut up
- 2 large-sized cucumbers, cut up
- 10 grams (¼ cup) fresh parsley, finely cut up
- 45 millilitres (3 tablespoons) fresh lemon juice
- 165 grams (1 cup) cooked chickpeas
- 2 large-sized tomatoes, cut up
- 60 millilitres (¼ cup) olive oil
- Salt and ground black pepper, as required

Directions:

1. Put cooked salmon and remnant ingredients into a bowl and blend to incorporate thoroughly.
2. Enjoy immediately.

Ground Beef & Cabbage Soup

Servings | 5   Time | 55 minutes
Nutritional Content (per serving):
Cal | 276   Fat | 10.2g   Protein | 34.3g   Carbs | 11.1g   Fibre | 3.3g

Ingredients:

- 15 millilitres (1 tablespoon) olive oil
- 455 grams (1 pound) ground beef
- 5 grams (1 teaspoon) salt
- 400 grams (4 cups) cabbage, shredded
- 2½ grams (½ teaspoon) dried thyme
- 2½ grams (½ teaspoon) dried oregano
- 1200 millilitres (5 cups) low-FODMAP beef broth

- 1 large-sized onion, cut up
- 2 garlic cloves, finely cut up
- 2½ grams (½ teaspoon) ground black pepper
- 1 (425-gram) (15-ounce) can diced tomatoes with juice
- 1 bay leaf
- 2½ grams 2½ grams (½ teaspoon) paprika

Directions:

1. Into a large-sized soup pan Put oil on burner and heat at around medium-high heat.
2. Cook the onion for around 3-5 minutes.
3. Put in the ground beef, garlic, salt and pepper and blend to incorporate.
4. Immediately turn the heat at around medium-high.
5. Cook for around 7-8 minutes.
6. Put in the cabbage, tomatoes, herbs, bay leaf, paprika and broth.
7. Cook the mixture until boiling.
8. Immediately turn the heat at around low.
9. Cook for around 25 minutes.
10. Blend in salt and pepper and enjoy hot.

Lentil Soup

Servings|6   Time|1 hour 35 minutes
Nutritional Content (per serving):
Cal| 103   Fat| 5.2g   Carbs| 12g   Fibre| 4.4g   Protein| 4g

Ingredients:

- 30 millilitres (2 tablespoons) olive oil
- 2 celery stalks, cut up
- 150 grams (¾ cup) brown lentils, rinsed
- 1¼ grams (¼ teaspoon) dried basil
- 5 grams (1 teaspoon) ground cumin
- 2½ grams (½ teaspoon) paprika
- 120 grams (4 cups) fresh spinach, cut up
- 30 millilitres (2 tablespoons) fresh lemon juice

- 2 carrots, peel removed and cut up
- 25 grams (¼ cup) green onion, cut up
- 600 grams (3 cups) tomatoes, finely cut up
- 1¼ grams (¼ teaspoon) dried oregano
- 2½ grams (½ teaspoon) ground coriander
- 1440 millilitres (6 cups) water
- Salt and ground black pepper, as required

Directions:

1. Sizzle oil on into a large-sized soup pan burner at around medium heat.
2. Cook the carrot, celery and green onion for around 6-7 minutes.
3. Put in lentils and cook for around 2-3 minutes.
4. Blend in the tomatoes, herbs, spices and water.
5. Cook the mixture until boiling.
6. Immediately turn the heat at around low.
7. Cook with the cover for around 1 hour.
8. Blend in the spinach, salt and pepper.
9. Cook for around 4-5 minutes.
10. Blend in the lemon juice and enjoy hot.

Pork Stew

Servings|10   Time|1 hour 40 minutes
Nutritional Content (per serving):
Cal| 276   Fat| 8.3g   Protein| 29 g   Carbs| 21.6g   Fibre| 4.2g

Ingredients:

- 910 grams (2 pounds) boneless pork roast, trimmed and cubed
- 100 grams (1 cup) green onion, cut up
- 4 medium-sized potatoes, peel removed and cubed
- 1 (510-gram) (18-ounce) can diced tomatoes
- 30 millilitres (2 tablespoons) balsamic vinegar
- 2 bay leaves
- 5 grams (1 teaspoon) dried oregano
- 155 grams (2 ounces) fresh oyster mushrooms, cut in half

- Salt and ground black pepper, as required
- 45 millilitres (3 tablespoons) olive oil
- 100 grams (1 cup) leek, thinly slivered
- 4 medium-sized carrots, peel removed and cut into ¾-inch pieces
- 840 millilitres (3½ cups) low-FODMAP chicken broth
- 5 grams (1 teaspoon) dried thyme
- 5 grams (1 teaspoon) dried basil
- 15 grams (½ cup) fresh parsley, cut up

Directions:

1. Put pork cubes, salt and pepper into a medium-sized bowl and toss to blend.
2. Sizzle oil into a large-sized Dutch oven on burner at around medium-high heat.
3. Cook the pork cubes in 2 batches for around 2-3 minutes.
4. Put the browned pork onto a plate.
5. Put green onion and leek into the same pan and cook for around 2-3 minutes.
6. Put in potatoes, carrots, tomatoes, broth, vinegar, bay leaves, thyme, oregano, basil, salt and pepper.
7. Cook the mixture until boiling.
8. Immediately turn the heat at around low.
9. Cook for around 5 minutes.
10. Put in the cooked pork.
11. Cook with the cover for around 45-50 minutes.
12. Put in mushrooms and cook for around 10-15 minutes.
13. Enjoy hot with the garnishing of parsley.

Shrimp Stew

Servings | 6   Time | 30 minutes
Nutritional Content (per serving):
Cal | 236   Fat | 11.1g   Protein | 26.6g   Carbs | 6.7g   Fibre | 1.2g

Ingredients:

- ❖ 30 millilitres (2 tablespoons) olive oil
- ❖ 40 grams (¼ cup) roasted red pepper, cut up
- ❖ 1 (400-gram) (14-ounce) can diced tomatoes with chilies
- ❖ 30 millilitres (2 tablespoons) Sriracha
- ❖ 30 millilitres (2 tablespoons) fresh lime juice
- ❖ 5 grams (¼ cup) fresh coriander, cut up
- ❖ 25 grams (¼ cup) green onion, cut up
- ❖ 680 grams (1½ pounds) shrimp, peeled and deveined
- ❖ 240 millilitres (1 cup) unsweetened coconut milk
- ❖ Salt and ground black pepper, as required

Directions:

1. Sizzle oil into a saucepan on burner at around medium heat.
2. Cook the green onion and red pepper for around 4-5 minutes.
3. Put in shrimp and tomatoes.
4. Cook for around 3-4 minutes.
5. Blend in the coconut milk and Sriracha.
6. Cook for around 4-5 minutes.
7. Blend in the lime juice, salt and pepper and take off from burner.
8. Garnish with coriander and enjoy hot.

Chickpeas Stew

Servings | 4   Time | 50 minutes
Nutritional Content (per serving):
Cal | 167   Fat | 5.2g   Protein | 7.7g   Carbs | 24.6g   Fibre | 5.8g

Ingredients:

- 15 millilitres (1 tablespoon) olive oil
- 300 grams (2 cups) carrots, peel removed and cut up
- 480 millilitres (2 cups) low-FODMAP vegetable broth
- 120 grams (4 cups) fresh spinach, cut up
- Salt and ground black pepper, as required
- 100 grams (1 cup) green onion, cut up
- 5 grams 5 grams (1 teaspoon) red pepper flakes
- 3 large-sized tomatoes, peel, seeds removed and finely cut up
- 125 grams (¾ cup) cooked chickpeas
- 15 millilitres (1 tablespoon) fresh lemon juice

Directions:

1. Sizzle oil into a saucepan on burner at around medium heat.
2. Cook the green onion and carrot for around 6 minutes.
3. Blend in the red pepper flakes and cook for around 1 minute.
4. Blend in the tomatoes and cook for around 2-3 minutes.
5. Blend in the broth.
6. Cook the mixture until boiling.
7. Immediately turn the heat at around low.
8. Cook for around 10 minutes.
9. Blend in the chickpeas and cook for around 5 minutes.
10. Blend in the spinach and cook for around 3-4 minutes.
11. Blend in the lemon juice and seasoning and take off from burner.
12. Enjoy hot.

Turkey & Beans Chili

Servings | 8   Time | 7 hours 20 minutes
Nutritional Content (per serving):
Cal | 302   Fat | 10.6g   Protein | 28.1g   Carbs | 30.2g   Fibre | 5.1g

Ingredients:

- 2 sweet potatoes, peel removed and cut up
- 50 grams (½ cup) celery stalk, cut up
- 2 (415-gram) (14½-ounce) cans diced tomatoes
- 120 millilitres (½ cup) water
- 15 grams (1 tablespoon) red chili powder
- 2½ grams (½ teaspoon) ground cumin
- 680 grams (1½ pounds) ground turkey
- 250 grams (1½ cups) cooked chickpeas

- 75 grams (½ cup) carrot, peel removed and cut up
- 1 (225-gram) (8-ounce) can low- FODMAP tomato sauce
- 2½ grams (½ teaspoon) ground cinnamon
- Salt and ground black pepper, as required
- 125 grams (1 cup) corn

Directions:

1. Sizzle a large-sized anti-sticking wok on burner at around medium-high heat.
2. Cook the turkey for around 8-10 minutes.
3. Take off the wok with the turkey from burner and drain the excess fat from the wok.
4. Put the cooked turkey, sweet potato, carrot, celery, tomatoes, tomato sauce, water and spices into a slow cooker and blend to incorporate thoroughly.
5. With the lid, cover the slow cooker and set on High for 5 hours, blending from time to time
6. Uncover the slow cooker and add in the corn and beans.
7. Again, cover the slow cooker and set on High for 1-2 hours further.
8. Enjoy hot.

Chickpeas & Courgette Chili

Servings|8   Time|1 hour 25 minutes
Nutritional Content (per serving):
Cal| 118   Fat| 4.5g   Protein| 4.1g   Carbs| 17.5g   Fibre| 4.3g

Ingredients:

- 30 millilitres (2 tablespoons) olive oil
- 1 large-sized capsicum, seeds removed and cut up
- Salt and ground black pepper, as required
- 600 grams (3 cups) tomatoes, cut up
- 480 millilitres (2 cups) water
- 2 celery stalks, cut up
- 5 grams (1 teaspoon) dried thyme
- 10 grams (2 teaspoons) cayenne pepper powder
- 2 large-sized courgettes, cut up
- 250 grams (1½ cups) cooked chickpeas

Directions:

1. Sizzle oil into a large-sized saucepan on burner at around medium heat.
2. Cook the celery and capsicum for around 8-9 minutes.
3. Blend in thyme, cayenne powder and salt and cook for around 1 minute.
4. Put in remnant ingredients and blend thoroughly.
5. Cook the mixture until boiling.
6. Immediately turn the heat at around low.
7. Cook for around 1 hour.
8. Enjoy hot.

Chicken & Broccoli Curry

Servings | 4   Time | 30 minutes
Nutritional Content (per serving):
Cal | 307   Fat | 16.4g   Protein | 34.3g   Carbs | 5.2g   Fibre | 1.9g

Ingredients:

- ❖ 30 millilitres (2 tablespoons) olive oil, divided
- ❖ Salt and ground black pepper, as required
- ❖ 100 grams (1 cup) green onion, cut up
- ❖ 225 grams (8 ounces) unsweetened coconut milk
- ❖ 4 (115-gram) (4-ounce) boneless chicken breasts, cut into small pieces
- ❖ 5 grams (2 teaspoons) fresh ginger, grated
- ❖ 135 grams (1½ cups) broccoli florets

Directions:

9. Sizzle half of oil into a large-sized wok on burner at around medium-high heat.
10. Stir-fry the chicken pieces, salt and pepper for around 4-5 minutes.
11. With a slotted spoon, transfer the chicken onto a plate.
12. Sizzle the remnant oil in the same wok on burner at around medium-high heat.
13. Cook the green onion and ginger for around 2-3 minutes.
14. Blend in the broccoli and stir-fry for around 3 minutes.
15. Blend in the cooked chicken and coconut milk.
16. Stir-fry for around 3-4 minutes
17. Blend in the salt and pepper and enjoy hot.

Parmesan Chicken Bake

Servings | 4   Time | 55 minutes
Nutritional Content (per serving):
Cal | 279   Fat | 11g   Protein | 37.9g   Carbs | 4.9g g   Fibre | 0.1g

Ingredients:

- 250 grams (1 cup) lactose-free yoghurt
- 4 (115-gram) (4-ounce) boneless, skinless chicken breasts
- 55 rams (½ cup) Parmesan cheese, grated
- Salt and ground black pepper, as required

Directions:

1. For preheating: set your oven at 190 °C (375 °F).
2. Line baking tray with a piece of heavy-duty foil and then spray it with baking spray.
3. Put the yoghurt, cheese, salt and pepper into a bowl and blend to incorporate.
4. Put the chicken breasts and coat with the yoghurt mixture.
5. Lay out the chicken breasts onto the baking tray.
6. Bake for around 45 minutes.
7. Enjoy hot.

Braised Chicken Thighs

Servings|6   Time|1 hour 10 minutes
Nutritional Content (per serving):
Cal| 441   Fat| 31.3g   Protein| 33.7g   Carbs| 3.9g   Fibre| 0.3g

Ingredients:

- ❖ 6 (150-gram) (6-ounce) bone-in chicken thighs
- ❖ 30 millilitres (2 tablespoons) olive oil
- ❖ 2 fresh dill sprigs
- ❖ 1 pinch of cayenne pepper powder
- ❖ 30 millilitres (2 tablespoons) fresh lemon juice
- ❖ 15 millilitres (1 tablespoon) cold water
- ❖ Salt and ground black pepper, as required
- ❖ 960 millilitres (4 cups) low- FODMAP chicken broth
- ❖ 2½ grams (½ teaspoon) ground turmeric
- ❖ 15 grams (2 tablespoons) arrow starch
- ❖ 5 grams (½ tablespoon) fresh dill, cut up

Directions:

1. Sprinkle the chicken thighs with salt and pepper.
2. Sizzle oil into a large-sized wok on burner at around high heat.
3. Put in chicken thighs, skin side down and cook for around 3-4 minutes.
4. Flip the thighs and add in the broth.
5. Arrange the dill sprigs over the thighs.
6. Sprinkle with cayenne pepper powder, turmeric and salt.
7. Cook the mixture until boiling.
8. Immediately turn the heat at around medium-low.
9. Cook with the cover for around 40-45 minutes, coating the thighs with cooking liquid.
10. Meanwhile, put arrow starch and water into a small-sized bowl and blend to incorporate thoroughly.
11. Discard the thyme sprigs and transfer the thighs into a bowl.
12. Put the lemon juice in sauce and blend to incorporate.
13. Slowly add arrow starch mixture, blending continuously.
14. Cook for around 3-4 minutes, blending from time to time.
15. Put the thighs and blend to incorporate.
16. Enjoy hot with the topping of cut up dill.

Ground Turkey with Veggies

Servings | 6   Time | 40 minutes
Nutritional Content (per serving):
Cal | 344   Fat | 19.4g   Protein | 35.2g   Carbs | 9.1g   Fibre | 3.1g

Ingredients:

- 680 grams (1½ pounds) lean ground turkey
- 225 grams (1½ cups) carrot, peel removed and cut up
- 300 grams (2 cups) fresh green beans, trimmed and cut into 1-inch pieces
- 1¼ grams (¼ teaspoon) red pepper flakes
- 30 millilitres (2 tablespoons) olive oil
- 5 grams (1 tablespoon) fresh ginger, finely cut up
- 60 millilitres (¼ cup) low-FODMAP chicken broth
- Salt and ground black pepper, as required

Directions:

1. Sizzle an anti-sticking wok on burner at around medium-high heat.
2. Cook the turkey for around 6-8 minutes.
3. With a slotted spoon transfer the turkey into a bowl and discard the spray from wok.
4. Sizzle oil in the same wok on burner at around medium heat.
5. Cook the carrot and ginger for around 5 minutes
6. Put the green beans and cooked turkey and blend to incorporate.
7. Put in broth, red pepper flakes, salt and pepper.
8. Cook the mixture until boiling.
9. Immediately turn the heat at around medium-low.
10. Cook for around 6-8 minutes, blending frequently.
11. Enjoy hot.

Herbed Flank Steak

Servings|6   Time|30 minutes
Nutritional Content (per serving):
Cal| 221   Fat| 9.5g   Protein| 31.6g   Carbs| 0.1g   Fibre| 0.1g

Ingredients:

- 2½ grams (½ teaspoon) dried thyme
- 2½ grams (½ teaspoon) dried parsley
- 680 grams (1½ pounds) flank steak, trimmed
- 2½ grams (½ teaspoon) dried oregano
- Salt and ground black pepper, as required
- Olive oil baking spray

Directions:

1. Put the dried herbs, salt and pepper into a large-sized bowl and blend to incorporate thoroughly.
2. Put the steaks and rub with herb mixture generously.
3. Set aside for around 15-20 minutes.
4. For preheating: set your grill to medium heat.
5. Spray the grill grate with baking spray.
6. Put the steak onto the grill over medium coals.
7. Cook for around 18-20 minutes, flipping once halfway through.
8. Take off the steak from grill and place onto a chopping board for around 10 minutes before slicing
9. Cut the steak into serving portions and enjoy.

Pork with Pineapple

Servings | 6   Time | 30 minutes
Nutritional Content (per serving):
Cal | 249   Fat | 8.7g   Protein | 30.6g   Carbs | 11.8g   Fibre | 1.3g

Ingredients:

- 30 millilitres (2 tablespoons) olive oil
- 5 grams (1 teaspoon) fresh ginger, finely cut up
- 155 grams (2 ounces) pineapple, cut into chunks
- 60 millilitres (¼ cup) fresh pineapple juice
- Salt and ground black pepper, as required
- 680 grams (1½ pounds) pork tenderloin, trimmed and cut into bite-sized pieces
- 2 large-sized capsicums, seeds removed and slices
- 45-60 millilitres (3-4 tablespoons) low-FODMAP chicken broth

Directions:

1. Sizzle oil into a large-sized wok on burner at around high heat.
2. Stir-fry pork pieces for around 4-5 minutes.
3. Transfer the pork into a bowl.
4. Sizzle remnant oil in the same wok on burner at around medium heat.
5. Cook the ginger for around 1 minute.
6. Blend in pineapple and capsicum and stir-fry for around 3 minutes.
7. Blend in pork, pineapple juice, broth, lime juice, salt and pepper.
8. Cook for around 3-5 minutes.
9. Enjoy hot.

Salmon Parcel

Servings | 6   Time | 35 minutes
Nutritional Content (per serving):
Cal | 224   Fat | 14g   Protein | 18.2g   Carbs | 8.2g   Fibre | 1.9g

Ingredients:

- ❖ 6 (85-gram) (3-ounce) salmon fillets
- ❖ 2 capsicums, seeds removed and cubed
- ❖ 1 small-sized onion, slivered thinly
- ❖ 30 millilitres (2 tablespoons) fresh lemon juice
- ❖ Salt and ground black pepper, as required
- ❖ 4 tomatoes, cubed
- ❖ 10 grams (½ cup) fresh parsley, cut up
- ❖ 60 millilitres (¼ cup) olive oil

Directions:

1. For preheating: set your oven at 205 °C (400 °F).
2. Arrange 6 pieces of foil onto a smooth surface.
3. Place 1 salmon fillet onto each foil piece and sprinkle with salt and pepper.
4. Put the capsicums, tomato and onion into a bowl and blend.
5. Place veggie mixture over each fillet and top with parsley.
6. Drizzle with oil and lemon juice.
7. Fold the foil around the salmon mixture to seal it.
8. Arrange the foil packets onto a large-sized baking tray into a single layer.
9. Bake in your oven for around 20 minutes.
10. Take off from the oven and transfer the foil packets onto serving plates.
11. Carefully unfold each packet and enjoy hot.

Haddock with Tomatoes

Servings | 2   Time | 30 minutes
Nutritional Content (per serving):
Cal | 244   Fat | 8.5g   Protein | 29.7g   Carbs | 12.5g   Fibre | 3.4g

Ingredients:

- ❖ 15 millilitres (1 tablespoon) olive oil
- ❖ 5 grams (3 tablespoons) fresh coriander, cut up
- ❖ 2 (115-gram) (4-ounce) haddock fillets
- ❖ 500 grams (2½ cups) tomatoes, cut up
- ❖ 15 millilitres (1 tablespoon) balsamic vinegar

Directions:

1. For preheating: set your oven at 165 °C (325 °F).
2. Sizzle oil into a medium-sized, ovenproof anti-sticking wok on burner at around medium heat.
3. Cook the tomatoes for around 2 minutes, blending continuously.
4. Blend in coriander and vinegar.
5. Cook for around 2-3 minutes.
6. Put in haddock fillet and blend to incorporate with sauce.
7. Transfer the wok into the oven and bake in your oven for around 12-15 minutes.
8. Enjoy hot.

Seafood Casserole

Servings | 8   Time | 1 hour 20 minutes
Nutritional Content (per serving):
Cal | 267   Fat | 17.9g   Protein | 22.9g   Carbs | 2.6g   Fibre | 0.4g

Ingredients:

- 600 millilitres (2½ cups) water
- 45 grams (3 tablespoons) unsalted butter
- 165 grams (1½ cups) cheddar cheese, shredded and divided
- 225 grams (½ pound) shrimp, peel removed and deveined
- 205 grams (1½ cups) crab meat, cut up
- 200 grams (2 cups) celery, cut up
- 240 grams (1 cup) heavy cream
- Salt and ground black pepper, as required
- 225 grams (½ pound) scallops, side muscles removed
- 220 grams (1½ cups) lobster meat, cut up

Directions:

1. For preheating: set your oven at 165 °C (325 °F).
2. Put the water into a large-sized saucepan at around medium-high heat.
3. Cook the water until boiling.
4. Put in the celery and cook for around 6 minutes.
5. With a slotted spoon, transfer the cooked celery into a large-sized bowl.
6. Put the scallops in the same pan of boiling water on burner at around low heat.
7. Cook for around 3 minutes.
8. With a slotted spoon, transfer the scallops into the bowl of celery.
9. Put the shrimp in the same saucepan of boiling water on burner at around low heat.
10. Cook for around 4 minutes
11. With a slotted spoon, transfer the shrimp into the bowl of celery.
12. Into another small bowl, reserve 180 millilitres (¾ cup) of cooking water and set it aside.
13. Put the lobster and crab meat into the bowl of shrimp mixture and blend thoroughly.
14. Sizzle the butter into a large-sized, flat-bottomed wok on burner at around medium heat.
15. Slowly put in the cream and reserved cooking water, whisking regularly to incorporate thoroughly
16. Cook for around 1-2 minutes.
17. In the saucepan, Put in 110 grams (1 cup) of cheese and blend until melted thoroughly.
18. Put in the seafood mixture, salt and pepper and take off from burner.
19. Put the mixture into a 9x13-inch baking pan and top with the remnant cheddar cheese.
20. Bake in your oven for around 35-45 minutes.
21. Take off the baking pan from oven and let it cool for around 5 minutes before enjoying it.

Noodles with Chicken & Veggies

Servings | 3   Time | 40 minutes
Nutritional Content (per serving):
Cal | 351   Fat | 7.5g   Carbs | 45.7g   Fibre | 4.1g   Protein | 26.2g

Ingredients:

- 45 grams (½ cup) broccoli florets
- 55 grams (1 cup) fresh kale, tough ribs removed and cut up
- 15 grams (1 tablespoon) coconut oil
- 1 (225-gram) (8-ounce) boneless, skinless chicken breast, cubed
- 75 grams (½ cup) fresh green beans, trimmed and slivered
- 150 grams (6 ounces) buckwheat noodles
- 100 grams (1 cup) green onion, finely cut up
- 60 millilitres (¼ cup) low-sodium soy sauce

Directions:

1. Put the broccoli and green beans into a medium-sized saucepan of boiling water.
2. Cook for around 4-5 minutes.
3. Put in kale and cook for around 1-2 minutes.
4. Drain the vegetables and transfer into a large-sized bowl. Set aside.
5. Put the noodles into another pan of lightly salted boiling water and cook for around 5 minutes.
6. Drain the noodles thoroughly and then, rinse thoroughly. Set aside.
7. Meanwhile, sizzle coconut oil into a large-sized wok on burner at around medium heat.
8. Cook the green onion for around 2-3 minutes.
9. Put the chicken cubes and cook for around 5-6 minutes.
10. Put the soy sauce and a little splash of water.
11. Cook for around 2-3 minutes, blending frequently.
12. Put in cooked vegetables and noodles.
13. Cook for around 1-2 minutes, tossing frequently.
14. Enjoy hot.

Snacks Recipes

Spiced Pecans

Servings|16 Time|20 minutes
Nutritional Content (per serving):
Cal| 125   Fat| 13g   Protein| 1.7g   Carbs| 2.4g   Fibre| 1.8g

Ingredients:

- 250 grams (2 cups) pecans
- 5 grams (1 teaspoon) fresh rosemary, cut up
- 5 grams (1 teaspoon) fresh oregano, cut up
- 1¼ grams (¼ teaspoon) cayenne pepper powder

- 30 millilitres (2 tablespoons) olive oil
- 5 grams (1 teaspoon) fresh thyme, cut up
- 2½ grams 2½ grams (½ teaspoon) paprika
- Salt, as required

Directions:

1. For preheating: set your oven at 175 °C (350 °F).
2. Line a large-sized baking tray with bakery paper.
3. Put pecans and remnant ingredients Into a bowl and toss to incorporate thoroughly
4. Transfer the pecan mixture onto the baking tray and spread into a single layer.
5. Roast for around 10-12 minutes, flipping after every 5 minutes.
6. Take off from oven and set the baking tray aside to cool thoroughly before serving.

Cinnamon Popcorn

Servings | 3   Time | 15 minutes
Nutritional Content (per serving):
Cal | 112   Fat | 9.5g   Protein | 1.3g   Carbs | 7.4g   Fibre | 1.2g

Ingredients:

- ❖ 30 grams (2 tablespoons) coconut oil
- ❖ 1¼ grams (¼ teaspoon) ground cinnamon
- ❖ 95 grams (¾ cup) popping corn

Directions:

1. Into a saucepan, melt coconut oil on medium-high heat.
2. Add popping corn and cover the pan tightly.
3. Cook for around 1-2 minutes, shaking the pan from time to time.
4. Take off the saucepan from burner and transfer into a large-sized heatproof bowl.
5. Add cinnamon and blend to incorporate thoroughly.
6. Enjoy immediately.

Banana Chips

Servings | 4   Time | 1 hour 10 minutes
Nutritional Content (per serving):
Cal | 61   Fat | 0.2g   Protein | 0.7g   Carbs | 15.5g   Fibre | 1.8g

Ingredients:

- ❖ 2 large-sized bananas, peel removed and cut into ¼-inch thick slices

Directions:

1. For preheating: set your oven at 120 °C (250 °F).
2. Line a large-sized baking tray with baking paper.
3. Put the banana slices onto the prepared baking tray into a single layer.
4. Bake in your oven for around 1 hour.

Sweet Potato Fries

Servings | 2   Time | 35 minutes
Nutritional Content (per serving):
Cal | 199   Fat | 14.3g   Carbs | 18.2g   Fibre | 3.5g   Protein | 1.8g

Ingredients:

- ❖ 1 large-sized sweet potato, peel removed and cut into wedges
- ❖ Salt and ground black pepper, as required
- ❖ 5 grams (1 teaspoon) ground turmeric
- ❖ 5 grams (1 teaspoon) ground cinnamon
- ❖ 30 millilitres (2 tablespoons) olive oil

Directions:

1. For preheating: set your oven at 220 °C (425 °F).
2. Line a large-sized baking tray with a piece of foil.
3. Put sweet potato wedges and remnant ingredients into a large-sized bowl and toss to incorporate thoroughly.
4. Transfer the potatoes onto the prepared baking tray and spread into an even layer.
5. Bake in your oven for around 25 minutes, flipping once after 15 minutes.
6. Take off from oven and enjoy immediately.

Deviled Eggs

Servings | 6   Time | 20 minutes
Nutritional Content (per serving):
Cal | 79   Fat | 5.1g   Protein | 6.9g   Carbs | 1.4g   Fibre | 0.2g

Ingredients:

- ❖ 6 large-sized eggs
- ❖ 5 grams (2 tablespoons) fresh chives, finely cut up

- ❖ 65 grams (¼ cup) lactose-free yoghurt
- ❖ 20 grams (1 tablespoon) Dijon mustard
- ❖ 1 pinch of cayenne pepper powder

Directions:

1. Put the eggs into a saucepan of water on burner at around high heat.
2. Cook the water until boiling
3. Cover the pan and immediately take off from burner.
4. Set aside with cover for at least 10-15 minutes.
5. Drain the eggs and let them cool thoroughly.
6. Peel the eggs and slice them in half vertically.
7. Take off the yolks from egg halves.
8. Carefully scoop out the yolks from each egg half.
9. Put the egg yolks and yoghurt into a mixer and process to form a smooth mixture.
10. Transfer the yoghurt mixture into a bowl.
11. Put the green onion, chives and mustard and blend to incorporate.
12. Spoon the yoghurt mixture in each egg half.
13. Serve with a sprinkling of cayenne pepper powder.

Almond Brittles

Servings | 8   Time | 25 minutes
Nutritional Content (per serving):
Cal | 123   Fat | 11.7g   Protein | 2.6g   Carbs | 2.7g   Fibre | 1.5g

Ingredients:

- ❖ 100 grams (1 cup) almonds
- ❖ 95 grams (½ cup) Erythritol
- ❖ 1¼ grams (¼ teaspoon) salt
- ❖ ¾ gram (1/8 teaspoon) coarse salt

- ❖ 55 grams (¼ cup) unsalted butter
- ❖ 10 millilitres (2 teaspoons) organic vanilla extract

Directions:

1. Line a 9x9-inch cake pan with bakery paper.
2. Put the butter, Erythritol, vanilla and 1¼ grams (¼ teaspoon) of salt into an 8-inch anti-sticking wok on burner at around medium heat.
3. Cook to incorporate thoroughly, blending continuously.
4. Blend in the almonds.
5. Cook the mixture until boiling, blending continuously.
6. Cook for around 2-3 minutes, blending continuously.
7. Take off the wok from burner and place mixture into the prepared pan.
8. With the back of a spoon, stir to spread the almonds and sprinkle with salt.
9. Set aside for around 1 hour.
10. Break into pieces and enjoy.

Parmesan Shrimp

Servings | 6   Time | 25 minutes
Nutritional Content (per serving):
Cal | 165   Fat | 8.8g   Protein | 21.7g   Carbs | 0.9g   Fibre | 0.1g

Ingredients:

- Olive oil cooking pray
- 30 millilitres (2 tablespoons) olive oil
- 2½ grams (½ teaspoon) dried oregano
- 455 grams (1 pound) medium shrimp, peeled and deveined
- 30 grams (¼ cup) Parmesan cheese, grated
- 2½ grams (½ teaspoon) dried basil
- Salt and ground black pepper, as required
- 30 millilitres (2 tablespoons) fresh lemon juice

Directions:

1. For preheating: set your oven at 205 °C (400 °F).
2. Lightly spray a baking tray with baking spray.
3. Put Parmesan, olive oil, herbs, salt and pepper and gently blend to incorporate.
4. Put in shrimp and toss to incorporate thoroughly.
5. Arrange the shrimp onto the prepared baking tray into a single layer.
6. Bake in your oven for around 6-8 minutes.
7. Take off the baking tray of shrimp from oven and drizzle with lemon juice.
8. Enjoy immediately.

Chicken Popcorn

Servings | 3   Time | 40 minutes
Nutritional Content (per serving):
Cal | 290   Fat | 21.4g   Protein | 18.2g   Carbs | 7.7g   Fibre | 2.9g

Ingredients:

- 225 grams (½ pound) chicken thigh, cut into bite-sized pieces
- 5 grams (1 teaspoon) ground turmeric
- 10 grams (2 tablespoons) coconut flour
- 15 grams (1 tablespoon) coconut oil, melted
- 200 grams (7 ounces) unsweetened coconut milk
- Salt and ground black pepper, as required
- 20 grams (3 tablespoons) desiccated coconut

Directions:

1. Put chicken, coconut milk, turmeric, salt and pepper into a large-sized bowl and blend to incorporate thoroughly.
2. Cover and put in your refrigerator to marinate overnight.
3. For preheating: set your oven at 200 °C (390 °F).
4. Put coconut flour and desiccated coconut into a shallow dish and blend to incorporate thoroughly.
5. Coat the chicken pieces in coconut mixture.
6. Arrange chicken pieces onto a baking tray and drizzle with oil.
7. Bake in your oven for around 20-25 minutes.
8. Enjoy moderately hot.

Berries Gazpacho

Servings | 6   Time | 10 minutes
Nutritional Content (per serving):
Cal | 77   Fat | 2.8g   Protein | 1.5g   Carbs | 13.3g   Fibre | 4.5g

Ingredients:

- ❖ 250 grams (2 cups) fresh raspberries
- ❖ 1920 millilitres (4 cups) unsweetened almond milk
- ❖ 300 grams (2 cups) fresh blueberries
- ❖ 2½ millilitres (½ teaspoon) organic vanilla extract

Directions:

1. Put raspberries and the remnant ingredients into a clean food processor and process to form a smooth mixture.
2. Enjoy immediately.

Stuffed Cherry Tomatoes

Servings | 12   Time | 20 minutes
Nutritional Content (per serving):
Cal | 45   Fat | 3.4g   Protein | 1.3g   Carbs | 3.1g   Fibre | 0.7g

Ingredients:

- ❖ 24 cherry tomatoes
- ❖ 20 grams (2 tablespoons) mayonnaise
- ❖ 10 grams (1 tablespoon) green onion, finely cut up
- ❖ 85 grams (3 ounces) cream cheese, softened
- ❖ 30 grams (¼ cup) cucumber, peel removed and finely cut up
- ❖ 5 grams (2 teaspoons) fresh dill, finely cut up

Directions:

1. Carefully cut a thin slice from the top of each cherry tomato.
2. With the tip of a knife, carefully take off the pulp of each cherry tomato and discard it.
3. Arrange the tomatoes onto paper towels to drain, cut side down.
4. Put the cream cheese and mayonnaise into a bowl and whisk to form a smooth mixture.
5. Put the cucumber, green onion and dill and blend to incorporate.
6. With a spoon, put the cheese mixture into each tomato.
7. Arrange the tomatoes onto a platter and refrigerate to chill slightly before serving.

Dessert Recipes

Lemon Sorbet

Servings | 4   Time | 10 minutes

Nutritional Content (per serving):

Cal | 127   Fat | 0.8g   Protein | 0.8g   Carbs | 29g   Fibre | 0.6g

Ingredients:

- ❖ 5 grams (2 tablespoons) lemon zest, grated
- ❖ 360 millilitres (1½ cups) fresh lemon juice
- ❖ 160 grams (½ cup) pure maple syrup
- ❖ 480 millilitres (2 cups) water

Directions:

1. Freeze ice cream maker tub for around 24 hours before making this sorbet.
2. Put lemon zest, maple syrup and water into a saucepan.
3. Cook them for around 1 minute, blending continuously.
4. Take off the pan from burner and blend in the lemon juice.
5. Transfer this into an airtight container and refrigerate for around 2 hours.
6. Now, transfer the mixture into an ice cream maker and process it according to the manufacturer's directions.
7. Return the ice cream to the airtight container and freeze for around 2 hours.

Blueberry Gelato

Servings | 6   Time | 25 minutes
Nutritional Content (per serving):
Cal | 89   Fat | 6.2g   Protein | 2.5g   Carbs | 6.6g   Fibre | 1.2g

Ingredients:

- ❖ 225 grams (1½ cups) fresh blueberries
- ❖ 480 millilitres (2 cups) unsweetened almond milk
- ❖ 4 large-sized egg yolks
- ❖ 1 pinch of salt

- ❖ 15 millilitres (1 tablespoon) fresh lemon juice
- ❖ 60 grams (¼ cup) heavy cream
- ❖ 145 grams (¾ cup) Erythritol
- ❖ 2½ millilitres (½ teaspoon) organic vanilla extract

Directions:

1. Put blueberries and lemon juice into a clean processor and process to form a smooth mixture.
2. Through a fine sieve, strain the blueberry mixture into a bowl by pressing with the back of a wooden spoon.
3. Discard the peel and set the puree aside.
4. Put the milk and cream into a saucepan on burner at around medium heat.
5. Cook the mixture until boiling.
6. Take off the saucepan of milk mixture from burner and set it aside.
7. Put in sugar and egg yolks into a bowl and with an electric mixer, whisk until yellow, pale and thick.
8. Add ¼ of the hot milk mixture and whisk to form a smooth mixture.
9. Put in the mixture into the pan with remnant milk mixture
10. Return the pan on burner at around low heat.
11. Cook for around 4 minutes, blending regularly.
12. Take off the pan of milk mixture from burner and immediately strain into a bowl.
13. Immediately put in vanilla extract, salt and strained blueberry puree.
14. Put in your refrigerator with cover overnight.
15. Put the blueberry mixture into an ice cream maker and freeze according to manufacturer's directions.
16. Put the ice cream into a sealable container and freeze until set thoroughly.

Berries Granita

Servings | 4   Time | 15 minutes
Nutritional Content (per serving):
Cal | 4   Fat | 0.3g   Protein | 0.7g   Carbs | 11.1g   Fibre | 2.8g

Ingredients:

- 125 grams (1 cup) fresh strawberries, hulled and slivered
- 20 grams (1 tablespoon) pure maple syrup
- 14-15 ice cubes

- 65 grams (½ cup) fresh raspberries
- 75 grams (½ cup) fresh blueberries
- 15 millilitres (1 tablespoon) fresh lemon juice
- 5 grams (1 teaspoon) fresh mint leaves

Directions:

1. Put the berries, maple syrup, lemon juice and ice cubes into a high-power mixer and process on high speed to form a smooth mixture.
2. Transfer the berries mixture into an 8x8-inch baking pan and freeze for at least 30 minutes.
3. Take off from the freezer and blend the granita thoroughly using a fork.
4. Return it to the freezer and freeze it for around 2-3 hours. Scrape it every 30 minutes with a fork.
5. Put the granita into serving glasses and enjoy immediately garnished with mint leaves.

Raspberry Mousse

Servings | 4   Time | 10 minutes
Nutritional Content (per serving):
Cal | 44   Fat | 0.8g   Protein | 1g   Carbs | 9.4g   Fibre | 5.1g

Ingredients:

- 315 grams (2½ cups) fresh raspberries
- 90 millilitres (1/3 cup) unsweetened almond milk
- 1¼ grams (¼ teaspoon) salt

- 70 grams (1/3 cup) granulated Erythritol
- 15 millilitres (1 tablespoon) fresh lemon juice
- 5 millilitres (1 teaspoon) liquid stevia

Directions:

1. Put raspberries and remnant ingredients into a clean food processor and process to form a smooth mixture.
2. Put the blended mixture into serving glasses and put in your refrigerator to chill before

3. enjoying it

Blueberry Pudding

Servings | 5   Time | 12 minutes
Nutritional Content (per serving):
Cal | 190   Fat | 11.7g   Protein | 2.7g   Carbs | 21.1g   Fibre | 2.3g

Ingredients:

- ❖ 240 millilitres (1 cup) unsweetened coconut milk
- ❖ 45 millilitres (3 tablespoons) fresh orange juice
- ❖ 5 grams (2 teaspoons) orange zest, grated very finely
- ❖ 225 grams (8 ounces) fresh blueberries
- ❖ 80 grams (¼ cup) maple syrup
- ❖ 5 millilitres (1 teaspoon) organic vanilla extract
- ❖ 15 grams (1 tablespoon) unflavored gelatin

Directions:

1. Put coconut milk and blueberries into a high-power mixer and process to form a smooth mixture.
2. Add maple syrup, orange juice and vanilla and process to incorporate thoroughly.
3. Through a fine sieve, strain the mixture into a saucepan on burner at around medium heat.
4. Cook for around 2 minutes, blending continuously.
5. Take off from burner.
6. Slowly put the gelatin and blend until dissolved thoroughly, blending continuously.
7. Lightly blend in orange zest.
8. Transfer the mixture into 4 serving bowls
9. Refrigerate to set before serving.

Cottage Cheese Pudding

Servings | 6   Time | 45 minutes

Nutritional Content (per serving):

Cal | 119   Fat | 8.5g   Protein | 8.3g   Carbs | 2.1g   Fibre | 0g

Ingredients:

- ❖ Olive oil baking spray
- ❖ 180 grams (¾ cup) heavy cream
- ❖ 180 millilitres (¾ cup) water
- ❖ 5 millilitres (1 teaspoon) organic vanilla extract
- ❖ 190 grams (1 cup) cottage cheese
- ❖ 3 eggs
- ❖ 95 grams (½ cup) granulated Erythritol

Directions:

1. For preheating: set your oven at 175 °C (350 °F).
2. Spray 6 (150-gram) (6-ounce) ramekins with baking spray.
3. Put cottage cheese and remnant ingredients into a clean processor and process to form a smooth mixture.
4. Put the blended mixture into the ramekins.
5. Lay out the ramekins into a large-sized baking pan.
6. Add hot water in the baking pan, about 1-inch up sides of the ramekins.
7. Bake in your oven for around 35 minutes.
8. Enjoy moderately hot.

Lemon Soufflé

Servings | 4   Time | 30 minutes
Nutritional Content (per serving):
Cal | 130   Fat | 7.7g   Protein | 10.4g   Carbs | 4g   Fibre | 0.2g

Ingredients:

- ❖ Olive oil baking spray
- ❖ 50 grams (¼ cup) granulated Erythritol, divided
- ❖ 5 millilitres (1 tablespoon) fresh lemon juice
- ❖ 5 millilitres (1 teaspoon) organic vanilla extract

- ❖ 2 large-sized eggs (whites and yolks separated)
- ❖ 220 grams (1 cup) ricotta cheese
- ❖ 5 grams (2 teaspoons) lemon zest, grated
- ❖ 5 grams (1 teaspoon) poppy seeds

Directions:

1. For preheating: set your oven at 190 °C (375 °F).
2. Spray 4 ramekins with baking spray.
3. Put egg whites into a clean glass bowl and whisk until foamy.
4. Add half of Erythritol and whisk until stiff peaks form.
5. Put ricotta cheese, egg yolks and remnant Erythritol into another bowl and whisk to incorporate thoroughly.
6. Put the lemon juice and lemon zest and blend to incorporate thoroughly.
7. Put the poppy seeds and vanilla extract and blend to incorporate thoroughly.
8. Put the whipped egg whites into the ricotta mixture and gently, blend to incorporate.
9. Put the mixture into the prepared ramekins.
10. Bake in your oven for around 20 minutes.
11. Take off from oven and enjoy immediately.

Egg Custard

Servings | 8   Time | 50 minutes

Nutritional Content (per serving):

Cal | 103   Fat | 3.8g   Protein | 3.8g   Carbs | 14.2g   Fibre | 0.4g

Ingredients:

- Olive oil baking spray
- Salt, as required
- 570 grams (20 ounces) unsweetened almond milk
- 1¼ grams (¼ teaspoon) ground cardamom
- 5 eggs
- 160 grams (½ cup) maple syrup
- ¼ grams (¼ teaspoon) ground ginger
- 1¼ grams (¼ teaspoon) ground cinnamon
- 1¼ grams (¼ teaspoon) ground nutmeg

Directions:

1. For preheating: set your oven at 165 °C (325 °F).
2. Spray 8 small ramekins with baking spray.
3. Put the eggs and salt into a bowl and whisk thoroughly.
4. Arrange a fine-mesh sieve over a medium-sized bowl.
5. Through a sieve, strain the egg mixture into a bowl.
6. Put in the maple syrup into the eggs and blend to incorporate.
7. Put in the almond milk and spices and whisk to incorporate thoroughly.
8. Put the blended mixture into the ramekins.
9. Lay out ramekins into a large-sized baking pan.
10. Add hot water in the baking pan about 2-inch high around the ramekins.
11. Bake in your oven for around 30-40 minutes.
12. Take off ramekins from oven and set it aside to cool.
13. Put in your refrigerator to chill before enjoying it.

Peanut Butter Fudge

Servings | 16   Time | 16 minutes
Nutritional Content (per serving):
Cal | 184   Fat | 15.9g   Protein | 6.9g   Carbs | 4.5g   Fibre | 3g

Ingredients:

- 360 grams (1½ cups) creamy, salted peanut butter
- 5 millilitres (1 teaspoon) organic vanilla extract
- 85 grams (1/3 cup) unsalted butter
- 130 grams 2/3 cup powdered Erythritol
- 1 scoop whey protein powder

Directions:

1. Put peanut butter and butter into a small-sized saucepan over low heat.
2. Cook until melted and smooth.
3. Put the Erythritol and protein powder and blend to form a smooth mixture.
4. Take off from burner and blend in vanilla extract
5. Put the fudge mixture onto baking paper-lined 8x8-inch baking pan and with a spatula, smooth the top surface.
6. Freeze for around 30-45 minutes.
7. Carefully transfer the fudge onto a chopping board with the help of the bakery paper.
8. Cut the fudge into equal-sized squares and enjoy.

Pumpkin Brownies

Servings | 9 Time | 55 minutes
Nutritional Content (per serving):
Cal | 61   Fat | 2g   Protein | 1.2g   Carbs | 11g   Fibre | 1.5g

Ingredients:

- 10 grams (1 tablespoon) ground flaxseeds
- 120 grams (½ cup) almond butter
- 80 grams (¼ cup) maple syrup
- 10 millilitres (2 teaspoons) organic vanilla extract
- 2½ grams (½ teaspoon) salt
- 30 millilitres (2 tablespoons) water
- 115 grams (½ cup) pumpkin puree
- 30 grams (¼ cup) unsweetened cocoa powder
- 2 grams (½ teaspoon) baking soda
- 5 grams (1 teaspoon) pumpkin pie spice
- 25 grams (¼ cup) dark chocolate chips

Directions:

1. For preheating: set your oven at 175 °C (350 °F).
2. Line a 6×6-inch baking pan with baking paper.
3. Put flaxseeds and remnant ingredients except the chocolate chips in the bowl of a food processor and process to form a smooth mixture.
4. Put the mixture into a large-sized bowl and gently Blend in chocolate chips.
5. In the bottom of the prepared baking pan, pour the brownie mixture.
6. With a spatula, smooth the top surface.
7. Bake in your oven for around 38-40 minutes.
8. Take off the baking pan with the brownie from oven and place onto a metal rack to cool thoroughly before cutting.
9. Cut the brownie into desired-sized squares and enjoy.

Blueberry Crumble

Servings | 5   Time | 55 minutes
Nutritional Content (per serving):
Cal | 129   Fat | 6.4g   Protein | 2g   Carbs | 16.8g   Fibre | 2.5g

Ingredients:

- Olive oil baking spray
- 3 grams (¾ teaspoon) baking soda
- 25 grams (2 tablespoons) coconut oil, melted
- 45 millilitres (3 tablespoons) water
- 225 grams (1½ cups) fresh blueberries
- 25 grams (½ cup) gluten-free oat flour
- 60 grams (¼ cup) unripe banana, peel removed and mashed
- 10 millilitres (2 teaspoons) fresh lemon juice

Directions:

1. For preheating: set your oven at 150 °C (300 °F).
2. Lightly spray an 8x8-inch baking pan with baking spray.
3. Put oat flour and remnant ingredients except the blueberries into a large-sized bowl and blend to incorporate thoroughly.
4. Put the blueberries in the bottom of the prepared baking pan and top them with the flour mixture.
5. Bake in your oven for around 40 minutes.
6. Enjoy moderately hot.

31 Days Meal Plan

Day 1:

Breakfast: Buckwheat Porridge

Lunch: Egg Salad

Dinner: Pork with Pineapple

Day 2:

Breakfast: Overnight Seeds Porridge

Lunch: Chicken Lettuce Wraps

Dinner: Chickpeas Stew

Day 3:

Breakfast: Oats & Quinoa Granola

Lunch: Egg Drop Soup

Dinner: Chicken Salad

Day 4:

Breakfast: Kale & Celery Smoothie

Lunch: Beef Burgers

Dinner: Chickpeas & Courgette Chili

Day 5:

Breakfast: Bulgur Porridge

Lunch: Stuffed Courgettes

Dinner: Turkey & Beans Chili

Day 6:

Breakfast: Salmon Omelet

Lunch: Raspberry Salad

Dinner: Herbed Flank Steak

Day 7:

Breakfast: Maple Pancakes

Lunch: Chicken & Veggie Kabobs

Dinner:

Day 8:

Breakfast: Salmon Omelet

Lunch: Tomato Soup

Dinner: Ground beef & Cabbage Soup

Day 9:

Breakfast: Green Veggies Quiche

Lunch: Scallops with Green Beans

Dinner: Lentil Soup

Day 10:

Breakfast: Tomato & Egg Scramble

Lunch: Stuffed Capsicums

Dinner: Chicken & Broccoli Curry

Day 11:

Breakfast: Banana Waffles

Lunch: Banana Curry

Dinner: Pork Salad

Day 12:

Breakfast: Strawberry Smoothie

Lunch: Beef Burgers

Dinner: Salmon Parcel

Day 13:

Breakfast: Blueberry Muffins

Lunch: Courgette & Tomato Salad

Dinner: Shrimp Stew

Day 14:

Breakfast: Strawberry Chia Pudding

Lunch: Spiced Ground Chicken

Dinner: Chickpeas & Courgette Chili

Day 15:

Breakfast: Chicken & Veggies Frittata

Lunch: Veggie Lettuce Wraps

Dinner: Chicken & Broccoli Curry

Day 16:

Breakfast: Strawberry Oatmeal

Lunch: Turkey Meatballs

Dinner: Pork Stew

Day 17:

Breakfast: Maple Pancakes

Lunch: Egg Drop Soup

Dinner: Braised Chicken Thighs

Day 18:

Breakfast: Strawberry Smoothie Bowl

Lunch: Spinach with Cottage Cheese

Dinner: Parmesan Chicken Bake

Day 19:

Breakfast: Cheese & Yoghurt Bowl

Lunch: Tofu with Broccoli

Dinner: Haddock with Tomatoes

Day 20:

Breakfast: Eggs with Beef & Tomatoes

Lunch: Stuffed Capsicums

Dinner: Pork Stew

Day 21:

Breakfast: Green Veggies Smoothie

Lunch: Chicken Gizzard with Cabbage

Dinner: Salmon Parcel

Day 22:

Breakfast: Oatmeal Yoghurt Bowl

Lunch: Egg Salad

Dinner: Seafood Casserole

Day 23:

Breakfast: Strawberry Chia Pudding

Lunch: Tomato Soup

Dinner: Braised Chicken Thighs

Day 24:

Breakfast: Banana Waffles

Lunch: Spiced Ground Chicken

Dinner: Lentil Soup

Day 25:

Breakfast: Acai Smoothie Bowl

Lunch: Raspberry Salad

Dinner: Ground Turkey with Veggies

Day 26:

Breakfast: Quinoa Porridge

Lunch: Turkey Meatloaf

Dinner: Herbed Flank Steak

Day 27:

Breakfast: Blueberry Muffins

Lunch: Veggie Lettuce Wraps

Dinner: Salmon Salad

Day 28:

Breakfast: Acai Smoothie Bowl

Lunch: Shrimp with Kale

Dinner: Pork Salad

Day 29:

Breakfast: Courgette Bread

Lunch: Turkey Meatloaf

Dinner: Shrimp Stew

Day 30:

Breakfast: Overnight Seeds Porridge

Lunch: Tofu with Broccoli

Dinner: Ground Beef & Cabbage Soup

Day 31:

Breakfast: Cheese & Yoghurt Bowl

Lunch: Shrimp with Kale

Dinner: Noodles with Chicken & Veggies

Printed in Great Britain
by Amazon